TALK BOURBON TO ME! 2

The Spirit of Hospitality

Beth Underwood

Copy editor: Joyce M. Gilmour, Editing TLC, www.editingtlc.com

Cover design: Darren Oliver

Unless otherwise noted, all images were taken by the author.

ISBN: 978-0-578-41691-5

A toast

To the visionaries of bourbon, and to all who have the courage to dream big dreams and see them through.

CONTENTS

FOREWORD

Who knew a course in geology freshman year at college would help educate me about two personal favorites: thoroughbred racing and bourbon?

Back then, "All I really need to know I learned in kindergarten," but we bourbon types like to think we're capable of achieving a higher education.

In learning about my local surroundings while in the bowels of Bowman Hall at the University of Kentucky, the subject of "Karst Geology" came to light. As water moves above and below the surface, it dissolves and erodes the limestone bedrock beneath the rich soils of Central Kentucky and Knobs Region. Putting limestone in the soil is a building block that helps young thoroughbreds develop, grow, and strengthen bone as they take nourishment out of the lush bluegrass. The area is also some of the best ground on the planet to grow the region's famous burr oak and pin oak trees, which create the canopies for the area's leading thoroughbred operations. And the limestone in the watershed is what helps give bourbon its unique flavor.

What a glorious spot on earth to be raised!

And what glorious fortune it has been to get fifty-one percent of my genes from my mother's side of the family considering my father's side was chockfull of teetotalers.

Every bourbon fan has their own story to tell. The trailhead of my personal bourbon journey is but a hazy memory, but as I recall it came at a time, like many Kentuckians, during those college days, and evenings…after geology class.

At the time the word "premium" was used for a brand of saltine crackers. The leading brands of the day were Early Times (with a garish yellow label), and Old Fitzgerald, Old Grand-Dad, Old Forester. History played a big role in the marketing budgets back then.

My father fancied Dowling 100, but my buddies and I landed on the Ezra Brooks brand. The price point was in our favor, and it conjured up a historical figure making good sour mash whiskey a century or so before, despite the fact the brand — made by Heaven Hill — came into existence in 1960.

All in all, it was probably the low point for bourbon consumers at the time, but Ezra Brooks helped a band of brothers from Central Kentucky celebrate the good victories of the University of Kentucky basketball teams and commiserate the losses piled up by the football squad throughout the 1980s.

In our day, before important sporting events, shots didn't "ring out"…they were poured.

For us the bourbon flowed at Commonwealth Stadium during football games, where having a date was essential—and one with a purse large enough to smuggle in a pint bottle of Ezra.

Along the way we learned to hone our palate. It took plenty of practice. One strong memory is sitting around someone's breakfast table, working our way through a fifth. Deep into the evening a pact was made that whoever had the first male child, he would be named "Ezra."

It's sad to report, eleven children later — six boys — none bear the name. Steadfast we weren't.

As the bourbon journey continued there was an awakening of sorts, as the market began to specialize and become "select."

As where once Maker's Mark was about the only "premium" bourbon on the shelf, the niche began to expand.

What a glorious time to be alive!

Moving away from Kentucky, then returning to settle in Woodford County while being named managing editor of *The Blood-Horse*, I began to "shop local" years before it became hip.

Blanton's came along in 1984, with its unique bottle, unique pricing, and a unique smoothness that had been missing from liquor store shelves. Brown-Forman unleashed Woodford Reserve in 1996 and it became an instant hit, not only locally on my shelf but also internationally. Bottles of Woodford would be used as barter/currency on trips to the Southern Hemisphere, much like Coors beer was to those of us east of the Mississippi in the 1970s.

As the closest distillery to our home in Versailles, it seemed only natural that Woodford Reserve would be the "house brand." Buffalo Trace, just a few miles farther down the road in Frankfort, become a go-to as well.

The flavors of Heaven Hill delight the senses; however, as a boy in Woodford County, isn't even sipping bourbon from Nelson County considered cheating?

In 2004 I plucked an assignment for *Keeneland* magazine to write about master distillers and their craft, and I was able to sit down and get personal with a select brotherhood of taste before they became rock stars: Woodford Reserve's Chris Morris, Parker Beam at Heaven Hill, and Buffalo Trace's Elmer T. Lee.

Morris explained the importance of nose: "Humans can detect 85 percent of flavor by the aroma," he told me. "People learn more things from their sense of smell than from any of the other senses."

He later explained his twelve-tier system of descriptions to break down the nuances in Woodford Reserve and a scorecard for each barrel.

Beam was succinct: "I don't equate bourbons to food. It's only supposed to taste like bourbon. You should taste the caramel from the wood, and then the grains that carry over, the things that give it the characteristics.

"I judge a good bourbon by how it finishes. A long, smooth finish. If I don't get that, then I don't like it."

What glorious stories we can tell!

Both bourbon lovers and fans of thoroughbred racing have a penchant for history. Both genres have plenty of lore from which to draw. Any employee of *The Blood-Horse* worth his or her salt has been taught about Joe Palmer, the former associate editor of the magazine and celebrated columnist for the New York *Herald Tribune*. His best work, columns about racing, drinking, and life, appear in "This Was Racing," published in 1953.

One standalone gem: "If you want to go to the Kentucky Derby, you may want to reflect thusly: four years ago this spring, two men, now unidentified, laid plans that are about to come to fruition. One planned the mating that led to the winner of the Kentucky Derby. The other was lighting the fire under the mash at the Brown Forman distillery. I say 'Strength to them both.'"

And here's to you, and the strength to continue along on your own personal bourbon journey.

—Evan Hammonds,
managing editor, *Blood-Horse*
October 2018

INTRODUCTION

Here we are again, back for the second in the *Talk Bourbon to Me* series, and it's a good one. Why? Because it's all about hospitality, in one form or another.

One would be hardpressed to find better hosts and hostesses than those of us in Kentucky. We like our Sunday dinners and summer barbecues, holiday gatherings and horse-themed galas.

We're natural entertainers.

Nowhere is that truer than at Kentucky's bourbon distilleries. Whether it's the front gate greeter or the retail manager, the tour guide, distillery owner, or master distiller, hospitality is the name of the game. Where else can you spend an hour with a stranger, share some bourbon, and come away with a new best friend? Nowhere, I tell ya.

With that in mind, I'd like to introduce you to a few of my new best friends — a sampling of bourbon's finest men and women who graciously shared their stories with me. Some have been in the bourbon industry for a few years, others a few decades. Regardless, one thing is clear: the spirit of hospitality they possess is as essential as the bourbon they produce. You're going to love these guys and gals!

As with the original *Talk Bourbon to Me*, I've added a few recipes I think you'll like, including an encore of the bourbon party mix featured in the first book. You'll also find a page for note-taking at the end of each chapter. Bring along the book when you visit distilleries and get your favorite master distiller to sign it. Paste in a sticker from the gift shop, or jot down thoughts during tastings.

For now, grab a glass of your favorite whiskey and let's talk bourbon!

PART ONE

Hospitality is defined as friendly, welcoming behavior toward guests or people you've just met — and here in Kentucky, we're no strangers to hospitality, especially when it comes to the bourbon industry.

According to the Kentucky Distillers' Association, Kentucky bourbon is an eight-and-a-half billion dollar industry that continues to flourish. This current period of unprecedented growth is underscored by more than a billion dollars in capital projects, whether recently completed, under way, or in the planning stages. What's more, each year more than a million people from all parts of the world travel to the Commonwealth for a taste of Kentucky bourbon culture.

That's a lot of hospitality.

I'm convinced it takes a certain breed of people to make that happen. After all, it's one thing to distill bourbon. It's quite another thing to barrel a spirit which in many cases won't be bottled for years, while asking the consumer to happily endure the wait right along with you. That takes some doing, not to mention a healthy dose of tenacity and perseverance, even audacity.

Ah, but that is the allure of bourbon — and the spirit of hospitality.

BETH UNDERWOOD

The Father of Bourbon Tourism

When people think of bourbon tourism, present-day distillery tours and festivals, branded T-shirts and barware often come to mind. Believe it or not though, the roots of bourbon tourism can be traced back more than 150 years. Bourbon was big business even then, evidenced by the thousands of distilleries in the Commonwealth.

Needless to say, there were plenty of movers and shakers in the bourbon world at that time, including Edmund Haynes "E.H." Taylor, Jr.

Because Colonel Taylor's legacy extends to multiple distilleries and various events, a quick overview of who he was and what he accomplished seems prudent.

With that in mind, I caught up with Brian Haara, Louisville attorney and bourbon history expert, who talked to me about Taylor's impact on the world of bourbon. Here's what I learned.

Let's get started with some background on Taylor. Born in 1830, he was the second cousin twice removed of America's

Photo courtesy of Buffalo Trace Distillery.

A banker and mayor of Frankfort on a number of occasions, Colonel Edmund Haynes Taylor Jr. was also a visionary in the Kentucky bourbon world.

twelfth president, Zachary Taylor (although many, Brian said, refer to Zachary as his great uncle). After his father died in 1835, some sources say the young Taylor and his mother lived with the future president in Louisiana for a time before moving back to Lexington, Kentucky.

Once back in the Bluegrass State, he was raised by his paternal uncle, Edmund Haynes Taylor, and in order to differentiate themselves, the two men added *Jr.* and *Sr.* to their surnames. Prior to the Civil War, the young Taylor followed in his uncle's footsteps and entered the banking business, although his career in banking was over by the time the war began.

"He traded tobacco and cotton during the war and didn't get into distilling until after the war," Brian said, noting that although he is known by many as Colonel Taylor, he was never in the military.

After the Civil War, he joined Gaines, Berry, and Company. The firm sent Taylor to Europe in 1866, where he gained extensive insights into the world of distilling. Upon his return, he drew from that experience to make great successes of Hermitage, Old Crow, and Old Pepper distilleries.

It's worth noting that at the time, his employer, which had reorganized as W.A. Gaines and Co. in 1868, was the largest producer of sour mash whiskeys in the world.

In 1870, he branched out on his own and purchased the Leestown Distillery on the banks of the Kentucky River in Frankfort, Kentucky. Today, this location is known as Buffalo Trace Distillery. Although the Leestown Distillery was already operational, the colonel made vast improvements, ultimately building the O.F.C. (Old Fire Copper or Old Fashioned Copper) Distillery.

"Colonel Taylor made the O.F.C. brand extremely popular and well known," Brian said. "The distillery was one of the top three most modern and showcase distilleries in Kentucky, along with the Hermitage and Old Crow — which, incidentally, were also projects overseen by Colonel Taylor."

Photo courtesy of Buffalo Trace Distillery.

Warehouse C, which bears the O.F.C. insignia, still stands at Buffalo Trace Distillery in Frankfort, Kentucky.

A marketer and salesman, innovator and visionary, Taylor had grand visions where the future of bourbon was concerned, and his work at the O.F.C. was only the beginning. As is par for the course though, the road to success is never straight — nor without a few potholes.

The financial crisis known as the Panic of 1873 ushered in six years of economic, civil, and employment unrest. Trouble was also brewing for Taylor, albeit by his own hands. And in 1877, things reached a boiling point for the colonel, who'd been doing some double dealing. As you can imagine, things didn't go well.

"He went bankrupt. He had to flee the country to avoid creditors, he sold the same barrels twice to different buyers," Brian said. "Everything he had built was crumbling down."

Lucky for us, another household name in the bourbon

world, George T. Stagg, bailed him out, even if Stagg's involvement was more calculated than benevolent.

"Stagg was shrewd," Brian noted. "He was a major (perhaps the largest) creditor of Colonel Taylor, and he made his move to take control of the O.F. C.

"One lawsuit I found in my research reported that Stagg paid twenty cents on the dollar to Colonel Taylor's creditors. Another lawsuit reported Colonel Taylor paid six cents cash on the dollar, and issued a promissory note for an additional seven cents on the dollar, which was guaranteed by Stagg. Either way, Stagg got an absolute deal in acquiring the O.F.C."

In the immediate years that followed, Brian said, Taylor and Stagg worked together at the O.F.C., and expanded with the Carlisle Distillery. And although the

Photo courtesy of Buffalo Trace.

Colonel Taylor's script signature was at the center of litigation for thirteen years. It can still be seen on every bottle of whiskey that bears his name.

name of their company was E.H. Taylor, Jr. Co., "Taylor only owned one share."

Nevertheless, Colonel Taylor's accomplishments and ties to O.F.C. are undeniable — Warehouse C still stands on the grounds of what is now Buffalo Trace.

"Warehouse C still stands as a testament to the grandeur that once existed at the property. Colonel Taylor built the O.F.C., then lost it, and then built his reputation back up after being financed by Stagg," Brian said. "But overall the O.F.C. held the low-point in Colonel Taylor's life. It was only after he left the O.F.C. that he became truly legendary."

Ten years later, on the first day of 1887, the two men officially parted ways. Moving forward, Stagg retained the O.F.C. and Carlisle Distilleries, while the U.S. Taylor Distillery in Millville went to the colonel.

"It was by far the smallest of the three distillery operations, and was (run) by Colonel Taylor's son, J. Swigert Taylor. That's

Public Domain photo

A venue for silent movies, posh parties, and fine bourbon, the Old Taylor Distillery in Millville, Kentucky was unlike anything the Commonwealth — or the bourbon world — had witnessed.

what became the Old Taylor Distillery in 1887," Brian said. "Colonel Taylor called his new enterprise E. H. Taylor, Jr. & Sons and he had to sue Stagg to prevent him from using the Taylor name."

That same year, Taylor took on the most ambitious distillery project of his career, building what became known as the Old Taylor castle. The structure — and the public's access to it — was like nothing the bourbon industry had seen. This

The Mark of a Colonel

Colonel Taylor's influence helped shape the bourbon industry, and even business law as we know it.

After Colonel Taylor and George T. Stagg parted ways, the colonel once again found himself in the courtroom. This time, he wasn't facing bankruptcy. He was facing his former partner, and seeking an injunction that would stop Stagg from using Colonel Taylor's script signature. That initial suit ignited more than a decade of legal disputes between the two bourbon legends.

"Taylor litigated against Stagg for thirteen years because Stagg continued to use Colonel Taylor's name," said Brian Haara, attorney and bourbon history expert. "In doing so, he helped establish significant trademark precedent."

The court ultimately sided with Colonel Taylor — and to this day, his trademark signature is easily recognizable on the bourbon that bears his name. The E.H. Taylor Jr. collection of whiskeys is produced at Buffalo Trace Distillery in Frankfort, Kentucky.

Unmistakable Influence

Colonel Taylor also helped pass the Bottled-in-Bond Act of 1897, which was the nation's first consumer protection law.

- He was instrumental in running rectifiers out of business and making those who stayed in business truthfully advertise their rectified whiskey.

- He made the Old Taylor brand famous across the nation.He created bourbon tourism and brought people to the Old Taylor Distillery.

- In 1917, he was awarded a "Master of Hospitality" degree by the American Association of Collegiate Registrars because of his reputation as quintessential host to all who visited the Old Taylor Distillery.

was the place where the colonel's mark on the industry took on new dimension, Brian said, and where the Old Taylor brand as we know it today originated.

"Although the Hermitage, Old Crow, and O.F.C. were also showpieces, they were nothing like the Old Taylor castle," Brian said, "and only the Old Taylor Distillery was designed to accommodate visitors."

The castle's pergolas, fountains, and sunken gardens attracted tourists from all over. Taylor even built his own station — Taylorton Station — so visitors could ride the train to the doors of the castle and spend the day picnicking and socializing on the distillery's opulent 113 acres.

Over the next twenty or so years, Colonel Taylor's reputation as an illustrative host continued to grow. He took

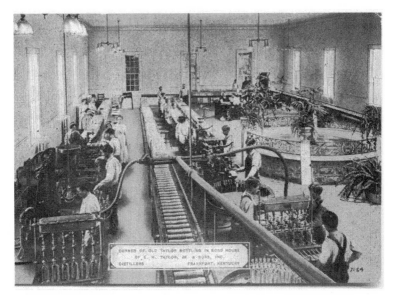

Public Domain photo

The Bottling in Bond House at the Old Taylor Distillery was not without luxury, as noted by the fountain at center right.

on a national role of sorts, playing an instrumental part in the Bottled-in-Bond Act of 1897 and the Pure Food and Drug Act of 1906 — both considered big wins for the bourbon consumers. He also held the distinction of being the first to bottle a million cases of straight bourbon. But as America's dry spell known as Prohibition swept the nation, the colonel's last days were close at hand. Colonel E.H. Taylor Jr., died in the winter of 1923.

His namesake, however, carried on.

"Old Taylor still had aging stocks in its warehouses during Prohibition which were sold by the American Medicinal Spirits Company, one of six recipients of a 'medicinal license' issued during Prohibition," Brian said. "This allowed the Old Taylor brand to continue to prosper despite Prohibition."

Once The Big Experiment ended in 1933, production

resumed at the castle under the National Distillers company.

"Old Taylor Distillery was so well built that it was able to go back into production upon Repeal," Brian said, "and it remained operational through 1972."

When the distillery went dark in 1972, the castle's best days appeared to be over, as the structures and grounds headed to a gradual — and seemingly irreversible — decline. The bottom had fallen out of the bourbon boom. Adults passed over the brown liquors in favor of clear spirits like vodka and gin.

National Distillers continued to use the warehouses for storage until it sold the Old Taylor Distillery and brand to Jim Beam in 1987.

"Beam, likewise, only used the warehouses until it sold the Old Taylor Distillery," Brian said.

In 2005, the property sold once again, this time to salvage investors. Pieces of the castle and warehouses — limestone, brick, and wood — were offered for sale, accompanied by certificates of authenticity. By most accounts, Colonel Taylor's story would appear to be over and done. But for reasons that can only be attributed to serendipity, his story is far from over.

Many thanks to Brian Haara for his input on this story. Brian has practiced law in Louisville, Kentucky for more than twenty years, currently as co-managing member of Tachau Meek PLC, a business litigation boutique firm, where he likes to think it's the type of firm Colonel E.H. Taylor Jr., would have hired for his overabundance of litigation. Recognized by Martindale-Hubble, Best Lawyers, and Super Lawyers, Brian's practice includes litigation of business (including bourbon trademark litigation), insurance, and real estate disputes.

The interplay between bourbon, law, and history led Brian to blog as Sipp'n Corn®, which quickly developed into media credentials, collaboration with retailers to select private barrels, and ultimately his forthcoming book, Bourbon Justice: How Whiskey Law Shaped America *(Potomac Books, 2018).*

"The water was not fit to drink.
To make it palatable, we had to add whisky.
By diligent effort, I learned to like it."

-Winston Churchill

UNEARTHING BOURBON POMPEII™

In 2016, less than ten miles away from the Old Taylor Distillery, plans were moving forward on a project at Buffalo Trace Distillery. The O.F.C. building, which had long been used for storage, was getting a complete overhaul on the way to becoming a new meeting and event space. But we all know that saying about best laid plans.

Here's a quick background on the building, which sits (literally) on the banks of the Kentucky River.

The original O.F.C. Distillery was built by our friend Colonel Taylor in 1869, then torn down in 1873 to make way for a larger distillery. This is, after all, Colonel Taylor we're talking about, and as we've seen, he was known to embrace the bigger-is-better mantra.

Flash forward a few years to 1882, when a lightning strike ignited a fire and destroyed the second building. As I'm sure you've surmised, the colonel wasn't easily deterred and wasted no time rebuilding once again.

This is key, though. Instead of tearing down what was left, he built a third distillery on top of the existing foundations.

As the years passed, fermenting processes outgrew the structure and were eventually moved to a another location on the property. In 1958, the fermenting vats were filled with dirt and concrete, and the building was decommissioned.

Now that you're up to speed, let's pick up back in 2016 and talk about that renovation project I was telling you about.

The first stage in the renovation included shoring up the foundation — as I mentioned earlier, the building sits right on the edge of the Kentucky River, and the risk of it toppling into the water wasn't an option.

Work was also under way on a new elevator shaft where workers came across something that caught their attention.

Photo courtesy of Buffalo Trace Distillery

The center fermenting vat has been lined with copper and is used for fermenting a select batch of bourbon.

And while their findings were not immediately clear, they weren't like anything they'd come across before.

It was a true stop-the-presses moment, which in a manner of speaking is exactly what the fine folks at Buffalo Trace did, bringing renovations to a screeching halt.

Realizing they were on the cusp of a major discovery, Historic Preservation Consultant and Whiskey Historian Carolyn Brooks and Bourbon Archaeologist Nick

A larger-than-life image of Colonel E.H. Taylor Jr. stands watch over the recently discovered ruins of the distilleries he built more than a hundred years ago.

Laracuente were called in to oversee what had turned into an excavation project. The distillery documented each step of the process as excavation teams continued to uncover partial walls and foundations from all three of Colonel Taylor's distilleries, as well as seven 11,000-gallon fermenting vats. Among the relics, they also discovered pieces of copper once used to line the massive vats. The site quickly became known as Bourbon Pompeii™.

Today, rows of green metal catwalks allow visitors to walk above the original distillery foundations and peer into the fermenting tanks for a rare look at distilling as it was done in the 1800s. In fact, one of the fermenters will soon be re-lined with copper (as Colonel Taylor would've insisted) and put back into action, allowing Bourbon Pompeii™ to become a working museum. I don't know about you, but that's a bottle of bourbon I can't wait to try.

While we're here at Buffalo Trace, you may have noticed the massive warehouse that greets visitors as they pull into the parking lot. That's Warehouse C, which we talked about earlier.

"He wanted it to be aesthetically pleasing, and of fine quality — something the people of the community would be

On site at what is referred to as Bourbon Pompeii™ at Buffalo Trace Distillery, visitors can get a real sense for 1880's distilling.

Inside Warehouse C, at Buffalo Trace Distillery. Keep your eyes open for some of the special barrels resting on the ricks.

proud of," said Freddie Johnson, VIP Visitor Lead at the distillery.

But there was more to it than looks alone. He hired structural engineers to get the job done right.

"Taylor believed if he built a structure of brick, mortar, and stone, it would be here for the long haul," Freddie said. "And he knew if he built it right, he could focus on making fine whiskey."

#bourbonlife

Early Espionage

If a distiller wanted to get a sample of a competitor's yeast strain, all he had to do was grab his walking stick, pay a visit to the distiller, and strike up a conversation.

"He'd say, 'Whatcha got going here?'" Freddie said. "At the same time, he'd poke it with his walking stick. That yeast would be right there on the stick, and that was all he needed."

Distillers also employed letter writing as a means to gain another distiller's yeast, Freddie said. In those early days, quarters were tight, the distiller's desk was often in close proximity to all the action, and yeast was everywhere.

"They'd write a letter that was guaranteed to elicit a response," he said, "and when the distiller wrote back, they'd steal the yeast by scraping it off the paper."

Once inside the massive brick and mortar warehouse, you'll notice two things: the ricks aren't attached to the building, making them earthquake tolerant, and they're made of red oak.

"Red oak leaks like a sieve," Freddie said, "but it's the last choice of termites."

Master Marketer

As the bigger picture on Colonel Taylor unfolds, we start to get a feel for his meticulous nature. From the structures he erected to the relationships he built, he left nothing to chance. Among his talents, he was also a master marketer.

In order to gain a following and increase demand for his product, he sent people to the bars of New York City. First, they'd put empty bottle sleeves on top of the trash. Next, one of them would go into the bar and request the product. After the product had been requested several times, the bar owners would seek out his product — which was easy, of course. All the bar owner had to do was look at the information on the empty sleeve.

"He was the king of promoting and brand recognition," Freddie said.

He was also the king of hospitality — and the party is just getting started.

> Around here, we have an open-door policy.
> You bring the bourbon and we'll open the door.

Buffalo Trace Distillery Visit

Notes:

_____
_____
_____
_____
_____
_____
_____
_____
_____
_____
_____
_____
_____

Buffalo Trace Old Fashioned

Here's a cocktail that seems fitting to honor Colonel Taylor. I'm sure you have all the ingredients on hand. If so, go ahead and mix it up. I'll wait
.

Ingredients:

- 50 ml Buffalo Trace Bourbon
- 1 sugar cube
- 2 drops Peychauds bitters
- Orange peel

Directions:

Place sugar cube, bitters, and orange peel in glass. Add half of the bourbon and crush the sugar cube. Add one ice cube and stir. Add more ice and the remaining bourbon and stir again. Garnish with dehydrated orange slice.

CASTLE & KEY

It was a perfect fall evening in Millville, Kentucky. A crowd of media representatives had gathered at what had once been known as Old Taylor Distillery to get a sneak peek at one of the most astounding transformations the Bluegrass State had known. For the first time in a hundred years, the grounds were alive once again with music and merriment, and the sounds of clinking glasses and chattering people filled the air. Even the yeast seemed to dance across the fermentation tanks with extra vigor.

The grand opening of the new Castle & Key Distillery was seven days away. By all accounts, *grand* wouldn't begin to describe what bourbon fans were about to witness.

On this day, it was easy to see how Colonel Taylor's trips to Europe had influenced his namesake with the Roman peristyle springhouse, English gardens, and Windsor-patterned castle. It was easy to envision life at the turn-of-the- nineteenth

Photos courtesy of Bill Straub, Modern Thirst (modernthirst.com)

Will Arvin and Wes Murry purchased the former Old Taylor Distillery in 2014, around the time these photos were taken. For more than forty years, the Old Taylor Distillery was left to ruin, overtaken by vegetation, wildlife, and vandals.

century — the tourists arriving by train at the property's Taylorton Station to attend lavish parties, picnic on the grounds, or view a silent movie, all the while enjoying fine bourbon whiskey.

What was difficult, though, was trying to imagine that less than four years prior to our visit, the property had been little more than a trash heap left to decay. More than forty years of overgrown brush and boarded up windows were accented with knee-deep piles of trash, broken beer bottles, and discarded mattresses. Nature's creatures staked their claim among the rust and disintegration. Then there was the structural damage,

Photo courtesy of Castle & Key Distillery

After four years of restoration and renovation, Castle & Key Distillery opened to the public in September 2018.

Photo courtesy of Castle & Key Distillery

The English gardens and a quarter mile walking trail were meticulously created by landscaped designer Jon Carloftis.

marked by collapsed roofs and rotting ricks. Prospective buyers walked away with tales of proverbial ten-foot poles.

But founding partners Will Arvin and Wes Murry saw the future where others saw futility. They purchased the property in 2014, and kicked off a four-year journey of revival.

With restoration under way, the men assembled a team of like-minded individuals to restore life to the grounds and open a new distillery. Castle & Key Distillery would become a destination reflecting the spirit of Colonel Taylor, while reimagining the future. Among the first brought in were master distiller Marianne Eaves — the first female in Kentucky to hold that title since prohibition — and landscape designer Jon Carloftis.

#distilledspirits

The Roman peristyle springhouse was built in the shape of a key. Colonel Taylor believed the spring was the key to his fine bourbon and his ultimate success.

Their shared belief in Castle & Key's vision was crucial in those early days of restoration — the state of the property was such that Marianne often referred to it as "a post-apocalyptic war zone."

But as dump truck after dump truck hauled away countless tons of garbage and debris, what was once left to ruin sprang back to life, piece by piece.

Photo courtesy of Castle & Key Distillery

Brass, copper, concrete, and wood combine to bring a feeling of old world luxury to the Boiler Room, which serves as a gift shop and tasting room.

Work began on the gardens first — they would serve as a source of inspiration for days when the way forward was muddied.

Not everything could be saved — Warehouse A was a casualty of years of neglect. Yet life still emerged when Jon created a botanical garden in its place. The herbs would flavor the spirits Marianne was creating, while bringing a renewed sense of order and purpose to the land.

At the far end of the property, the fate of a 534-foot aging warehouse — the longest of its design in the world — was also at stake. While consultants advised to tear it down, local tobacco barn builders believed it could be saved. Over the course of two years, they did just that, rebuilding fifty percent of the ricks in the process.

So go the myriad stories of how a group of knights in shining armor salvaged an abandoned castle. On this particular evening, it appeared as if a half-century of neglect had been a bad dream. And for all who'd believed it couldn't be done, the transformation was nothing short of miraculous.

Maybe it was a miracle. As for me, I'd like to think of it as the beginning of a happily ever after — a bourbon fairy tale come true.

While many distillery cats are busy chasing mice, Rick the cat spends most of his time dealing with matters of hospitality and exceptional guest experiences. Based on his attire, that should come as no surprise.

Castle & Key Distillery Visit

Notes:

Castle & Key's Gin & Tonic

While we're waiting for their first bourbon to be released, here's a fitting cocktail that will serve us well, don't you think?

Ingredients:

- 1.5 oz. Castle & Key Gin
- .5 oz. Jack Rudy Classic tonic syrup
- 3 oz. club soda

Mix ingredients in a cocktail shaker and serve over ice. Garnish with a lemon peel and dried juniper berries.

PART TWO

Now that we have a good sense of how bourbon tourism took root, let's take a brief look at the process of distilling and the rules of the game. There's no better place to do this than school, of course — in this case, a school for distilled spirits. What's that, you say? A school for distilled spirits? You bet! Without this basic knowledge, we can't expect to be model hosts and hostesses.

From there, we'll do a deep dive into two parts of the bourbon-making process. First, we'll take a look at yeast. Yeast is arguably one of the most baffling facets of the whiskey-making process, at least for people like me who don't naturally excel at things like science. Based on the number of people who've echoed my sentiments, I'm not alone.

We'll round out this second part with a look at a couple of Kentucky's coopers. These days, we see a boatload of aftermarket products made from barrels. Yet it's easy to overlook how fundamental they are to bourbon's beginnings. Without the cooper's barrels, we'd have no way to age, or enhance, our bourbon.

BETH UNDERWOOD

MOONSHINE UNIVERSITY

The Greek biographer and essayist Plutarch once said, "The very spring and root of honesty and virtue lie in good education." He's right, you know. And a proper education into the world of distilled spirits is no exception.

Until 2012, however, the art — and science — of distilling wasn't taught in the United States. At least not formally, anyway. The how-tos, whys, whens, and wheres were picked up from reading books or observing the methods of the distillers. Not an overly daunting task for those already in the business of distilling. But for the non-experienced with a dream of opening a distillery, no single place existed to impart the vast knowledge needed to run a successful distillery.

Enter Moonshine University — and the Stave & Thief Society.

Photo courtesy of Moonshine University

The courses at Moonshine University are hands-on — some of the work takes place inside the on-site distillery.

Since opening its doors in 2012, Moonshine University has hosted students from across the United States and thirty-five countries around the world.

Located in Louisville, Kentucky, or as many refer to it, the Napa Valley of Bourbon, Moonshine University has assimilated more than fifty faculty members — experts in every aspect of distilling — who are dedicated to sharing their knowledge on the art and science of distilling, and best practices for success.

But wait, there's more. In addition to providing an educational facility, Moonshine U also houses its own artisan distillery for hands-on training. Moreover, it's the exclusive education provider for the Kentucky Distillers' Association. Pretty impressive, if you ask me.

Among their eighteen courses offered, the flagship "6-Day Distiller Course" takes students through a complete overview of owning and running a craft distillery, providing materials, hands-on instruction, and networking opportunities with fellow distillers as well as other leaders in related industries, such as contractors and equipment manufacturers, branding experts, scientists, and legal consultants.

But one needn't be opening a distillery to benefit from Moon U. Another arm of Moonshine University deals with the hospitality side of things. And as you know, *Talk Bourbon 2* is all about hospitality.

The Stave & Thief Society, founded in 2014, is host to the Executive Bourbon Steward (EBS) course. Originally a program to raise bourbon knowledge for the hospitality industry, it was opened to all bourbon enthusiasts in 2015. It's

From left, Janeen, David and Irene, my fantastic flight-building partners at Moonshine University.

The coveted Executive Bourbon Steward challenge coin. Don't leave home without it.

the only bourbon education course which has been approved by the Kentucky Distillers' Association, and it is required of all distilleries and sponsors entering the Kentucky Bourbon Trail® and the Kentucky Bourbon Trail Craft Tour ®.

As an Executive Bourbon Steward, I can tell you from first-hand experience: it is the best way to forward your knowledge of distilled spirits. It's a full day of hands-on, intense training — flight building and sensory training and mash cooking and heads and tails cutting. And there's a test —which you must pass.

If you can stick with it though — and of course you can, right? — you'll gain membership into the exclusive Stave & Thief Society. You'll also be qualified to share your knowledge with others. At a time when bourbon is more popular than ever, there's also plenty of false information floating around out there. It'll be up to you to spread the truth — and to make sure you always have your Executive Bourbon Steward challenge coin with you, lest you be charged with buying my drink when we run into each other at a bar.

For more information on Moonshine University, Stave & Thief Society, and the courses and programs offered, contact the registrar at (502) 301-8139 or visit their websites: www.moonshineuniversity.com and www.staveandthief.com

The Basics of Bourbon and Rules of the Game

In the world of bourbon, some things bear repeating, especially when it comes to the rules of the game. So let's do a quick rundown on six requirements needed for bourbon to be bourbon:

- Must be at least fifty-one percent corn.
- Must be produced in the United States.
- Must be placed in a new charred oak barrel. Typically, the oak will be white American oak. But it doesn't have to be.
- Must be distilled to less than 160 proof.
- Must enter the barrel at 125 proof or less.
- Must have nothing added to it other than water.
  Remember, none of the above are negotiable.

Here are few more things to keep in mind:
- There are no stipulations on aging. As long as the spirits are poured into a new charred oak barrel, they can be poured right back out again. The caveat? An age statement. As of 2017, anything aged under four years must have an age statement.
- Straight bourbon must be aged for two years or more.
- Kentucky bourbon must be produced and aged at least one year in Kentucky.
- Bottled in bond means a bourbon was made in one distillery, in one season, aged for at least four years, and bottled at 100 proof.

- Bourbon does not have to be made in Kentucky. That said, about ninety-five percent of bourbon comes from the Commonwealth.

The History of the "e"

If you've paid much attention to whiskey bottles, you've noticed whiskey can be spelled two ways—with an "e" and without an "e". Generally speaking, if the place of origin has an "e" in its name—think Ireland, for example—whiskey will be spelled with an "e". On the other hand, Scotch whisky won't have the "e".

That said, it stands to reason, American whiskey would include the "e", right? Well, most of the time. As most things go, though, there are exceptions to every rule — Makers Mark, Old Forester, and George Dickel among them. Rebels, I tell ya!

Flavor Profiles

A long list of factors can affect the flavor of your favorite bourbon. Among them:

- The height the barrel is stored at — first floor versus fifth, for example.
- Location in the warehouse — north wall, east wall, or smack dab in the middle, for example.
- Temperature control, or lack thereof.
- Humidity levels.

Speaking of, the cooler the climate, the more mellow and smooth the bourbon. The hotter the climate, the spicier or more robust it will be.

By getting to know about the qualities of corn, rye, wheat and barley prior to distillation, the whiskey drinker can identify their presence in the final product.

When acquiring a taste for bourbon (or any distilled spirit, for that matter), it's important to remember there are no wrong answers.

"Whatever you smell or taste is what you smell or taste," says Moonshine U's Director of Spirits Education, Colin Blake. And like anything else, repetition is the key to mastery. "It pulls on experience. The more you do it, you get better and quicker at pulling the flavors out."

So, what exactly should you be looking for?

Corn: Unless the bourbon aged for less than a month or two — which is possible, although perhaps not advisable—the true corn flavor will be gone. But the sweetness from the corn will remain.

Wheat: Look for nutty, creamy, buttery flavors, and a mellow taste.

Rye: Think spicy — even minty — bright and bold.

What makes Kentucky bourbon so special?

Many Kentuckians will tell you bourbon is special for no other reason than because it was a gift from Heaven — that all the stars aligned and the blessings of caramel-colored nectar rained down on the Commonwealth at large, blessing the entire state as if we won the lottery. And that could be partially true.

Here in Kentucky, we have a lot going for us in the natural resources department — other blessings if you will. Things like:

- Water. The water that goes into our bourbon flows over a bed of limestone. The limestone filters the water and removes the iron. It also adds nutrients that help feed the yeast.

- Oak. Here in Kentucky, it just so happens we're situated among a vast expanse of oak trees, perfect for all those barrels we use.

- Soil. Kentucky's soil is the perfect breeding ground for grains — especially corn.

- Seasons. If ever there was a place where one could experience the four seasons, it's here in Kentucky. Wild swings in the temperature, coupled with the fluctuating barometric pressure are commonplace, sometimes within the course of twenty-four hours! (I like to refer to these days as winter coat mornings and swimsuit afternoons.) Those seasonal changes over the months and years affect how the bourbon intermingles with the barrel.

- Yeast. Yeast is thick in the Commonwealth's air — well, anyone's air for that matter. Especially in years past, distilleries relied on wild fermentation. Today, it's a whole new ballgame. Which leads us to our next host...

DID YOU KNOW?

If we lined up every aging barrel of Kentucky bourbon, they would stretch all the way from Portland, Maine to Portland, Oregon — and 136 miles into the ocean.

Put another way, that's a stack of shot glasses high enough to make it to the moon — and three-quarters of the way back. And it's 4.5 drinks for every man, woman, and child in the state of Kentucky. But who's counting. Right?

DERBY FAVORITE

Kentuckian Renea Terhune is a die-hard horse lover, bourbon drinker, and lover of everything Bluegrass. Not only does she have a sharp eye for the horses, she also has exquisite taste, evidenced by the following recipe.

From Renea: "I learned this one at a mixology class at Keeneland. It's my favorite horse-inspired bourbon drink, and was given to me by Fran Stalcup. Enjoy!"

What you'll need:

Highball glass

Shaker with ice

Build the drink in shaker:

1.5 oz. bourbon

1 oz. Triple Sec

2 oz. pineapple juice

Fresh lemon squeeze

3 dashes orange bitters

Shake hard and strain over ice. Garnish with lemon round.

Another empty bourbon bottle and still no genie at the bottom.

I'll keep looking.

talkbourbon.com

THE SCIENCE OF YEAST

Of all the pieces of the distilling puzzle — and there are more than a few — yeast is non-negotiable when it comes to making our favorite whiskey. Here's the dirty little secret, though: I don't know about you, but my vast understanding of yeast is about as clear as mud. No wonder I don't get calls for sourdough bread starters.

With that in mind, I wanted to enlist the help of a true yeast expert. So I called on Dr. Pat Heist, who along with Shane Baker, owns Ferm Solutions, as well as Wilderness Trail Distillery in Danville, Kentucky.

Ferm Solutions collects and markets both fuel ethanol and beverage alcohol yeasts, and supplies hundreds of distilleries, both in the United States and around the world. They're also

Dr. Pat Heist is co-founder of Ferm Solutions and Wilderness Trail Distillery in Danville, Kentucky.

industry leaders in yeast and bacteria research and development. If anyone knows yeast, it's these guys.

Pat, who's a self-proclaimed microbiologist at heart, has been studying, producing, identifying and analyzing yeast and bacteria for about thirteen years now. So I asked him to help me gain a better understanding of our favorite single-celled microorganisms. "Animalcules," as our ancestors referred to them.

Talk Bourbon: Can you give us a little history on yeast?

Pat: Making fermented beverages and bread dates back to before written languages, like 5,000 B.C. or before. But it wasn't until the invention of the microscope and the work of early microbiologists that yeast was even discovered. The microscope was first invented in the late 1500s and the first meaningful use of the microscope wasn't until the late 1600s. Louis Pasteur is credited with discovering and explaining the fermentation process and how it involved yeast, which wasn't until the 1850s.

Bread making was probably the root of how people started understanding yeast. Old distillers' books refer to a bread dough (probably more like a cross between mash and bread dough) for storing yeast strains.

Talk Bourbon: Looking back a hundred or more years, how could distillers tell if they had the right yeast or the wrong yeast?

Pat: I'd say if they made good alcohol and it tasted good, they knew they had the right yeast. It's likely that bad product or failed fermentations would have been frequent due to things like poor understanding of enzymes and starch conversion, bacterial contamination, temperature control, and general cleaning and sanitation, among others. These are things we can control now.

Talk Bourbon: Once a distiller discovered a good batch of yeast, how did he hold on to it?

Pat: In early U.S. history, whiskey makers would store yeast as leftovers from a previous batch. The vessels they used for this were these very durable copper jugs you could tightly

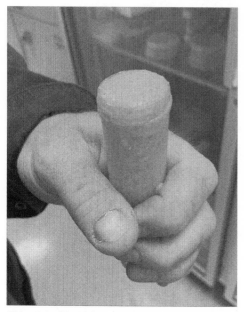

This vial of healthy yeast bubbled up and out of the tube within a split second of hitting fresh air.

seal. Most of them had a valve and spigot on the top for dispensing the yeast. These were reportedly attached to a string and sunken to the bottom of a lake or well to keep them cool and safe.

Distillers were said to have taken yeast jugs home with them in case the distillery burned down or the yeast strain was otherwise lost (or in case they got fired). I'm not a whiskey historian, but that's what I've heard about the old yeast jugs.

Talk Bourbon: Let's say I found a dried-out yeast jug that had been sitting around for years. Is it possible to pull the yeast from that old yeast jug?

Pat: Yes. We have done more than one project looking at old yeast jugs. We've successfully extracted DNA and have been able to match up an old yeast strain based on its DNA sequence.

Talk Bourbon: Speaking of DNA, how did you guys get your start?

Pat: I have an agricultural background and received my bachelors, masters, and Ph.D. from the University of Kentucky. I worked at a medical school and did some consulting. I'm a microbiologist at heart. I met my business partner, Shane, when we played together in a local band. Shane is a mechanical engineer and has an extensive background in business management, so we were the perfect match for starting Ferm Solutions back in 2006. Our focus was on fuel ethanol plants because they purchase large quantities of yeast and other products, but today our core business serves both fuel and beverage alcohol producers.

We know from our research, yeast that make alcohol are present on grains and fruits as well as other areas of the environment (air, water, etcetera), but so are a lot of other microbes that you don't want — mainly bacteria. When we first

The facilities at Ferm Solutions hold about 6,000 yeast isolates, and about 15,000 bacterial isolates.

started Ferm Solutions, to get new strains we would go out and buy different fruits (grapes are a great choice), mash them up like you would do for wine, maybe add a little water and extra sugar. You'll start getting carbon dioxide production and some of the crude fermentations will take off.

From the ones that smelled great and had an alcoholic odor, we would run more sophisticated lab tests like HPLC (High Performance Liquid Chromatography) to determine alcohol production, sugar utilization, organic acid production (all the hallmarks of a good distiller's yeast). From the satisfactory batches we would culture the yeast, isolate as pure cultures and from there begin more specific testing like fermentation in different substrates — such as grain, sugar, molasses, etc. Or we would do genetic fingerprinting to see how one yeast compared to another. Once we have the yeast

According to chemistry, whiskey is a solution.

in pure culture, we freeze it away for long-term storage in cryogenic freezers kept at minus eighty degrees Centigrade.

Talk Bourbon: About how many different strains of yeast are in your collection? Do you have a favorite story about any of the yeast you've worked with/discovered? Or the yeast that got away?

Pat: We estimate our collection to hold about 6,000 different yeast isolates. Many of them are the same species (*Saccharomyces cerevisiae*, for example), but the collection has a lot of diversity — some of the yeast have not been previously described. We are in the process of characterizing all the yeast in our collection, which involves identifying to species level, reviewing literature to see what, if anything, is known about them and then evaluating for utility in fuel or beverage alcohol production or even non-alcoholic fermented beverages like kombucha and kefir. Furthermore, some of the strains can be used to ferment industrial waste to produce fuel or beverage alcohol, things like leftovers from the orange juice process, expired bakery goods, cheese and yogurt whey, among others.

One of my favorite yeast stories involves us matching up an old family yeast strain from DNA we isolated from an old copper yeast jug. Some people call Ferm Solutions the CSI of Bourbon! We use all the experience and knowledge gained at hundreds of distilleries over more than a decade and put it into Wilderness Trail Distillery. Try our Wilderness Trail Bourbon and you'll see what I mean!

Talk Bourbon: Anything else we need to keep in mind when it comes to yeast and our beloved bourbon?

Pat: Just remember as you are enjoying your favorite Bourbon and thinking about the grain recipe, the limestone filtered water and the great flavors the barrel contributes, at the heart of the entire process is the yeast that is not only responsible for every drop of alcohol in the bottle, it is also a

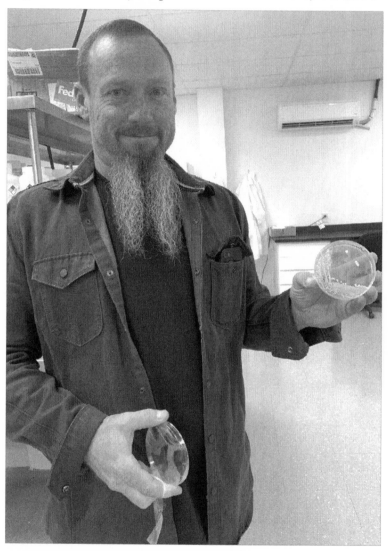

Dr. Pat Heist, a microbiologist at heart, with one of the thousands of yeast cultures at Ferm Solutions.

significant contributor to the flavor, mouthfeel and many other aspects of why we love Bourbon so much.

Bourbon Forensics

Every distillery, young and old, will have their own set of contaminants that are normally bacteria and what we call "wild yeast" (a yeast that got into the fermenter without your help). One of Ferm Solutions specialties is to know which contaminants are the good guys, and which are the bad guys, both in terms of alcohol production, and flavor.

"It's kinda like going to the doctor when you're sick," Pat said. "The doctor determines what's wrong, what's causing the problem, then prescribes the best treatment to get rid of the problem."

In matters of distilling, yeast gets the blame for practically every problem a distiller has, he said.

"Early on, we knew we had to become experts in the entire alcohol production process, which is different for fuel and beverage alcohol as well as beer or wine. We had to be able to help a customer get to the bottom of the issue whether it be from poor grain quality, enzymatic conversion of starch to fermentable sugars, fermentation issues, bacterial contamination, and the like, so when our yeast got the blame, we could point the customer in the direction of the solution. That's the foundation of our business, to help our customers to make the best product possible with the best yeast strains available.

In addition to Ferm Solution's yeast expertise, Wilderness Trail Distilling is the nation's fourteenth largest bourbon distiller. Their impact on the world doesn't stop there, though. Just as we mentioned that all bacteria isn't bad, there's more than one use for it, as well. It just so happens most bacteria that cause problems in fermentation (Ferm Solutions estimates they have about 15,000 bacterial isolates), are the same bacteria that are currently being marketed as "probiotics." Now Pat and Shane and their team of scientists are working toward probiotics for people, cattle, dogs, and horses.

"You never know how life will twist and turn," Pat said.

Oh so true. I suspect as long as there are experts like these guys around, there will never be a dull moment in the world of yeast and bacteria. And there certainly wouldn't be all the fine bourbon we've come to know and love without them.

Ferm Solutions and Wilderness Trail Distillery are located at 4095 Lebanon Road in Danville, Kentucky. For additional information, visit Ferm-Solutions.net or WildernessTrailDistillery.com

Cash Cows

We all know good bourbon takes time. In order to earn an income, early distillers often grew crops and raised livestock on their land to offset the wait needed to age the whiskey. That way they were making cash from the corn or the pigs or the cows they sold. Ergo the term "cash cow."

Wilderness Trail Distillery Visit

Notes:

Bread Pudding with Bourbon Sauce

Here's a tasty recipe for bread pudding that comes from the folks at Maker's Mark®.

Ingredients:

- 4 large eggs
- 2 ½ cups heavy whipping cream
- 1 ¾ cups dark brown sugar
- ¾ cup semi-sweet chocolate chips
- 1 loaf white bread

For the sauce:

- 2 cups brown sugar
- 1 cup heavy whipping cream
- 3 oz. (2 shots) Maker's Mark® or favorite bourbon, or to taste

Mix eggs, cream, and sugar well. Dice the bread and add to egg mixture along with the chocolate chips and stir. Cover and refrigerate overnight. When ready to bake, preheat oven to 350° F. Grease an 8"x8" pan and place parchment paper halfway up on all sides. Pour in pudding mixture, cover with parchment paper and foil. Bake for 90 minutes, uncover and bake an additional 15–20 minutes. A slight jiggle should remain.

For sauce:
Mix brown sugar and whipping cream in a sauce pan. Bring to a boil, stirring continuously, and remove from heat. Add bourbon to taste and stir.

Spoon into serving dishes and serve warm, and top with caramel sauce.

We all need something
to believe in.
I believe I'll have
some bourbon.

BETH UNDERWOOD

THE STORY OF BARRELS

As you may know, bourbon is a relatively new phenomenon — the term wasn't even bantered about until the 1800s.

The barrels in which it is stored, however, have a long and interesting past, dating back to ancient Babylon where casks made from cane and wood were used to transport wine. Other forms of open-ended barrels were around then, too — usually hollowed-out logs or crude buckets covered with animal hide.

Flash forward to 300-500 B.C, and the Iron Age, and we find the Celts are credited with the invention of barrels as we know them.

The Celts also discovered iron. So in addition to iron weapons like javelins and swords, the Celts also had access to iron tools, which came in handy when working with the abundance of European oak. Since that time, few changes have been made to the overall design — and barrels were long considered the prime way to store and transport goods.

Why barrels? Several reasons. They stack easily, can tolerate stress, and pound-for-pound they're much easier to move around because of their shape. Once on its side, a barrel can be rolled with relative ease — an important point consi-dering an empty barrel weighs more than 100 pounds and a full barrel weighs more than 500 pounds.

They've been used for storing olives and oils, flour and food, weapons and wine, to name but a few. There's also the matter of magic that occurs when the alcoholic spirits bathe in its hollow belly. But you know that already.

The Cooper's Craft

Here in bourbon country, there's a valid argument to be made that a cooper's job is as important as that of the distiller. Without the cooperage, bourbon would have no place to age — no place to develop its distinct personality.

You may be wondering, though: *What exactly is a cooper?*

I'm glad you asked. A cooper is one who crafts and/or repairs all those wood barrels that ultimately hold our favorite spirits. Needless to say, there's a lot riding on the cooper and his expertise.

Oddly enough, no formal training is available — no Bill's School of Barrel-making, for example. Instead, the craft is taught old school, requiring all aspiring coopers to apprentice under a master cooper for three to five years.

While that tutelage is a great start, the master cooper will concede that the learning never ends. After all, turning an oak tree into a booze-worthy barrel isn't as easy as it looks. And if you ask me, it doesn't look easy at all.

The history of coopers is as old as the barrels themselves. Their skills were in high demand, and masters of the craft were sought after worldwide for hundreds if not thousands of years.

But in the middle of the twentieth century, plastics, cardboard, and other forms of containers hit the market and the trade of coopering took a huge hit. By the 1970s, coopering looked to become a dying art, at least in the western world.

Why? Because another shift was taking place. People were ditching their whiskey for liquors like vodka, which require no aging, much less a barrel. Whether the younger generation was turning their collective back on the drinks their parents enjoyed, or all the world wanted to be more like James Bond and his shaken-not-stirred axiom, vodka sales surpassed whiskey sales in 1973.

The decline continued for almost a quarter-century. Some of Kentucky's bourbon distilleries closed almost immediately. Others hung on as long as possible. No one escaped unscathed—including the coopers, whose well-honed skills were left to atrophy.

As the first decades of the 21st century unfolded, a strange and wonderful anomaly took shape, and the world of bourbon whiskey began its ascent from the ashes.

Maybe it was blessed by the natural ebb and flow of the universe. Or perhaps it was a long overdue return to the roots and traditions of Kentucky's Commonwealth — a nod to the rich soil and limestone streams and the corn crops that sustained those early settlers.

Whatever the catalyst, one thing is certain: as long as spirits are aged in a barrel, the master cooper will be as sought after as the spirits that inhabit his barrels.

Britney Wimsatt, director of craft sales and marketing at Kelvin Cooperage.

Kentucky's Cooperages

Here in Kentucky, we have a number of cooperages — all of whom have their own ways of making spirits happy.

At this point, you may be wondering why you haven't heard as much about cooperages as distilleries. It's because a cooper's work is often done behind closed doors. Not because they're sworn to secrecy (at least I don't think they are!) but because it's a dangerous job: wood chips and sparks flying through the air, massive controlled fires in the bellies of the barrels, and workers tossing around more than a hundred pounds of hard wood like they were tossing foam balls. Trust me, you don't want to tangle with a barrel.

Let's be honest, though, where there's danger, there's also a certain mystique — a special je ne sais quoi — that no doubt lends itself well to the world of bourbon.

Enter Kelvin Cooperage.

Originally founded on the banks of the River Kelvin in Glasgow, Scotland, Ed McLaughlin opened his cooperage in 1963 after a five-year apprenticeship. He moved the family business to Louisville in 1991. Today, Ed's sons, Kevin and Paul, run the cooperage. And in most respects, they run things just like Ed ran them.

Britney Wimsatt, director of craft sales and marketing, said, "It's like stepping back in time to a Scottish cooperage as it would've been years ago."

To some, it may seem labor intensive — which isn't to say they don't also employ state-of-the-art equipment when fitting. But the fine folks at Kelvin Coop-erage don't believe in short cuts, especially if it compromises the end result.

Each barrel has somewhere in the neighborhood of thirty staves. It's similar to putting together the pieces of a puzzle. The cooper is looking for the perfect fit to create a tight seal.

"To do things the way they would've been done back then — to have that in a society where there's so much focus on instant gratification — that's something you don't see a lot of," Britney said.

Blending time-honored coopering traditions with state-of-the-art technology has earned them a reputation for quality and service that brings in customers across the country and around the world.

From Portland to Pakistan and Argentina to Israel, the folks at Kelvin Cooperage welcome representatives from a host of other countries—and the cultures they bring with them. For example, when a shipment of barrels is headed to Israel, a rabbi must bless all of the Jewish barrels to make sure they're kosher.

"A barrel can literally be passed around the world and used for decades, which is fascinating to me," Britney said. "The beauty of this concept is not only the green environmental impact, but the opportunity to learn, understand, and impact other cultures is incredible."

At the end of the day, it's more than a barrel. It's a relationship. It's an intangible part of the process that can't be automated. Nor should it be.

"Even before the whiskey has hit the barrel, we're able to have a positive impact on the consumer's experience," Britney said. "And that's pretty special."

Coopers and Hoopers

Back in the day, coopers had assistants, called hoopers. Guess what they did. That's right — they fitted the hoops

#alligatorchar

around the barrels. It was their sole job. This isn't always rocket science, thank goodness.

At some point, the coopers must have decided hoopers were overrated, and absorbed the job of hooping.

Chars & Toasts

At this point, you already know the first rule of bourbon. It must enter a new charred oak barrel.

Kelvin Cooperage uses real wood fires to char and toast their barrels.

But there's another step along the way that you may not be aware of.

"The toast is where all the flavor is," said Kelvin Cooperage's Britney Wimsatt. As the spirits age and the weather changes for example, the spirits seep through the char and into the toast, instilling additional layers of flavor. "The deeper the toast level, the better."

During the barrel-making process, char and toast levels can be customized as desired by the distiller, further adding to distinct flavor profiles.

Unlike charring, which takes only a matter of seconds, the toasting can take up to twenty minutes.

The many lives of bourbon barrels

I think we can all agree those oak barrels lead a charmed life — some are lucky enough to accommodate bourbon for twenty years or more. But once that last drop of bourbon leaves the cask, most barrels still have a lot of life left in them.

"The process of using and reusing barrels is much like using a tea bag," said Aaron Willett, who's the cooperage manager at Speyside Cooperage.

Who knew Tabasco Brand Pepper Sauce was aged in whiskey barrels?

For our purposes, of course, the first cup of tea is bourbon. After the bourbon is dumped, there's plenty of life left in the barrel, just like there's life left in a used tea bag. For many, that's the sweet spot.

"Some people prefer that second or third cup of tea from that bag," he added.

That's where places like Speyside come into play. Although they make new oak barrels at their Ohio plant, their Kentucky location specializes in repairing the used barrels and getting them back on the market for other aging purposes — wine, scotch, and even Tabasco sauce.

"A used barrel cooperage is basically a recycling center,"

said Aaron Willett, cooperage manager. "We have to find a way to utilize used or broken materials."

Much like every other aspect of bourbon, recycling is part art and part science.

Once a barrel is dumped at a distillery, the clock starts ticking. It's on a short timeline to make it back to a cooperage.

"It's a two- to three-day turnaround from the time a barrel is dumped until it's at our door," Aaron said. Considering they receive a whopping 1,500 to 2,000 barrels a day, there's never a dull moment.

Speyside Cooperage receives 1,500 to 2,000 barrels a day. From there, it's a race against the clock to make needed repairs and get them out the door again.

Once the barrels arrive, the clock keeps running. For the cooperage, that means a two- to four-week window to get the barrel back into circulation — not only are the barrels perishable, there's also the issue of pliability. The longer the belly of the barrel stays dry, the more the wood dries out, meaning the staves become less pliable and the work of the cooper is much tougher.

After the barrel undergoes needed repairs, it can have fifty to eighty years ahead of it to continue creating and enhancing the flavors of everything from whiskey and wine to honey and coffee — and everything in between.

As the years pass, though, it takes more time to extract flavor from the barrel. When the flavor is gone, the life of the barrel comes to an end, too. Some even return to the soil— literally — and are cut in half, filled with dirt, and decorated with plants.

These days, though, there's so much more that can be done with a used barrel. After the world of distilling has bid the barrel farewell, American ingenuity goes to work, creating a host of aftermarket products from the individual barrel parts. Staves become tasting flight holders or coat racks, heads become Lazy Susans, hoops become light fixtures. The opportunities are limited only by the imagination — and the barrel parts are in high demand.

To satisfy that demand, Speyside sells aftermarket products both wholesale and to the public, with barrel parts going to everything from smokehouses to furniture makers.

"This is the second oldest industry in the world," Aaron said. "I think it was never gonna go away, but it's definitely reemerged in the public eye. There's no doubt about that."

Spicy Pickles, a.k.a. The Tabasco Pickle Hack

While most of us don't have empty bourbon barrels sitting around, we do have access to Tabasco Brand Pepper Sauce, which just so happens to be aged in those used barrels. Give this recipe a try the next time you're looking to add some spice to life.

INGREDIENTS
25 oz. jar of pickles
1 T. Tabasco Original Red

DIRECTIONS

Open pickle jar and add one tablespoon of Tabasco Original Red. Close lid tightly, and shake to incorporate. Use right away for light heat/flavor, or let sit in the fridge for a few days to develop more heat and flavor.

#toastthetrees

Photo courtesy of Father Jim Sichko

Pappy for Pope Francis

When we consider all the natural resources that come together to create a great bottle of bourbon, can anyone doubt divine intervention? I think not. How appropriate, then, that a Kentucky priest bestow a few bottles of liquid sunshine on the pope himself.

In the spring of 2018, Father Jim Sichko, who hails from the Lexington, Kentucky Diocese, was part of a Kentucky contingent bound for Italy. I'm sure it goes without saying, an opportunity to meet with Pope Francis was a big deal — and Father Sichko couldn't arrive empty handed, right?

But what on earth could one present to the head of the Catholic Church? It's a quandary that could've stumped a lesser man. Fortunately for Pope Francis, Father Jim is a gift-giving virtuoso whose generosity and charitable heart is well documented. So it should come as no surprise that Father Jim chose to bring the pope bourbon — and not just any bourbon, mind you. He presented the pontiff with a bottle of (uber-rare) 23-year-old Pappy Van Winkle.

The gift-giving didn't stop there, though. Father Jim also brought along some Four Roses, Woodford Reserve, and Knob Creek. Sounds like I need to invite Father Jim to my next party.

Survey Says...

A while back, I sent out a survey to people on the *Talk Bourbon to Me* Facebook page (note: if you aren't already a part of this group, jump over and join. I'll wait.) It may not be the most scientific survey out there, but it's fun to see how people responded. In all, forty-five people took time to answer the five questions I posed. Here's what they had to say:

- Forty-four percent of bourbon drinkers enjoy bourbon in a variety of ways — neat, on the rocks, in a cocktail, you name it. Twenty-nine percent prefer it on the rocks, while only thirteen percent drink it neat. Eleven percent go the cocktail route, while a rogue two percent don't even like bourbon. Which begs the question, why bother with the survey?

- More than fifty percent of respondents spend between twenty-five and sixty dollars a bottle. Twenty-two percent say price isn't a factor. Eighteen percent spend twenty-five dollars or less, while nine percent said they'll most likely spend more than fifty dollars a pop.

- When deciding on what bourbon to buy, thirty-one percent will choose from something they sampled at a distillery, twenty-two percent go with small batch, and twenty percent go with single barrel selections. Rounding things out, only four percent were in the high rye crowd, while thirteen percent went for a wheated selection. Another twenty percent choose a little of this and that, making choices based on other factors — something they tried with a friend, recommendations of others, etc.

- Forty-three percent say they've toured about six distilleries, while thirty-six percent have visited one or two. Only thirteen percent have never done a tour — and nine percent say they've done them all.

BETH UNDERWOOD

PART THREE

While the bourbon ages in those oak barrels, I wanted to bring you a selection of, shall we say, spirited conversations with a few more folks whose daily lives revolve around liquid sunshine. Some of the faces may be familiar, while others are relative newcomers to the Kentucky bourbon scene — and remember, new in bourbon years can mean a handful of years. Regardless, all of them are enhancing the industry in their own unique way. I am honored to have made their acquaintances.

Let's meet them now.

BETH UNDERWOOD

The greeter known 'round the world

"The best part of my day is waking up every morning, going to work, and meeting people from all around the world. It's the greatest job I've had."

If you've paid a visit to Stitzel-Weller Distillery in Shively, Kentucky, chances are good you had the pleasure of meeting Carroll Perry. In fact, he's likely the person who greeted you as you drove onto the property.

Perry started at the distillery in September 1970, not long after returning from Vietnam. Now seventy-four, he marked his forty-eighth year at the distillery in September 2018.

"Back then, you had to work for sixty days before you

became a perm-
anent employee,"
he said, noting his
first job there was
in advertising. "A
lot of times, they'd
let you work fifty-
nine and a half
days, and let ya go."

Through the
years, Perry held
several jobs at the
distillery, ranging
from the warehouse
department to security.

No visit to Stitzel-Weller is complete until you've met Carroll Perry.

"I trained little Julian VanWinkle (Julian VanWinkle III) in that warehouse right there," he said with a smile, pointing directly across the street from the gatehouse where he greets visitors.

"In 1999, I tried to retire," he said. But his retirement was short lived. "I got called back in 2000 to train new staff, and have been here ever since as a greeter."

Even with all his past experience at the distillery, nothing could've prepared him for the bourbon craze that was about to take hold.

"I've been around distilleries most of my life. Right now is the biggest boon I've ever seen."

As surprising as the bourbon craze though, are the people

#Iheartbourbon

drinking it.

"When I was growing up, you couldn't hardly get a lady to take a drink of bourbon. The young ladies love it now."

These days, he's comfortable in his role as greeter extraordinaire and chief security ambassador, achieving a certain degree of notoriety.

He's been in commercials for Proof Media, and

Carroll Perry and I posed for an obligatory photo under the street sign that bears his name. "In all of my seventy-two years I have been in the industry, never did I dream I would have a street named after me," he said.

at one point had more hits on Yelp than anyone in the Commonwealth of Kentucky. He's recognized by people from around the world.

"One day a couple from Austria came through, and the lady kept looking at me. 'You're Perry!' she finally said. 'Your picture is in every bar in Austria!'"

Although the recognition is nice, Perry's true satisfaction is found at the small guard shack located on the right as visitors turn onto Perry Lane.

"The best part of my day is waking up every morning, going to work, and meeting people from all around the world," he said. "It's the greatest job I've had."

Tom Bulleit looks to the future

The Bulleit Distilling Company has been a dream of mine ever since I was in college, working in Kentucky distilleries in between school terms. I fell in love with the industry, and wanted to be a master distiller like my uncle. You could say bourbon has always been in my blood. Twenty years later, that dream ultimately became a reality when I started Bulleit Bourbon based on a historic family recipe on March 14, 1987. For many years, I was selling Bulleit by hand from

Photo credit: Bulleit Frontier Whiskey Experience at Stitzel-Weller.

bar-to-bar, and thanks to persistence and the relationships built with bartenders early on, Bulleit has become one of the fastest growing American whiskeys today.

We celebrated the thirtieth anniversary with a ribbon-cutting ceremony for the Bulleit Distilling Company in Shelbyville, Kentucky, which also happened to be my birthday and my wedding anniversary with my lovely wife Betsy. It was incredible to see how life has come full circle now that we have opened a new distillery for Bulleit Bourbon. We couldn't have made it this far without the tireless commitment of all the men and women who believed in Bulleit.

Bulleit has been my life's work and the Bulleit Distilling Company has been an ongoing project for us. Currently we're building a visitor center and look forward to opening our doors to friends from across the world in 2019.

Stitzel-Weller Distillery Visit

Notes:

Bourbon Marinade

This is a super simple and tasty marinade for your favorite cut of beef. I've never used it with pork or chicken, but I'm betting it would be delish!

Ingredients:

1 cup water
2/3 cup good bourbon
½ cup soy sauce
¼ cup packed brown sugar
3 T. Worcestershire sauce
2 T. lemon juice
1 T. minced garlic

Directions:

Place meat in a plastic zipper bag. Whisk together all ingredients and pour over meat. Seal bag, squeezing out any excess air as you zip it up. Marinate for eight hours or overnight.

Grill or cook using your favorite method.

Bourbon is an
acquired taste.
If you don't like it,
you should acquire
some taste.

Through the looking glass

I've always been drawn to rabbit holes — to following a trail into the unknown, entertaining thoughts and conversations with no preconceived outcome, taking risks that stretch the boundaries of possibility. So when I learned Rabbit Hole Distillery was coming to Louisville, visiting was a no-brainer.

I met Rabbit Hole founder Kaveh Zamanian in late spring, a month or so before the distillery opened to the public. Whether it was the architecture, the conversation, or the distilled spirits talking — perhaps a combination of the three — I knew right away Rabbit Hole Distillery was going to live up to its name.

Born in Iran and raised in California's wine country, Kaveh told me he'd been living in Chicago, running a successful clinical practice, and enjoying the Scotch whiskey he'd long enjoyed when fate stepped in. He fell in love with a Kentucky

When Kaveh Zamanian entered the distilling industry, he jumped into the proverbial "rabbit hole" with both feet — and he hasn't looked back.

belle — and the bourbon she introduced him to — and there was no turning back.

When the idea for a distillery began to take shape, he focused on creating an experience that would educate, elevate, and entertain guests.

"I was tired of seeing the same thing everywhere," Kaveh said. "I saw an opportunity to do something unique."

Instead of a building on a vast expanse of Kentucky bluegrass, Kaveh chose an urban setting. In relative terms, the distillery's footprint is small — about fifty-five thousand square feet. The structure was designed in the style of modernist architect Ludwig Mies van der Rohe, who created spaces based on their function. From concrete and copper to glass and steel, every element is intentional, chosen for its unique role in the distillation process. The end result is something to behold. Wide walkways

As visitors begin their ascent through Rabbit Hole Distillery, they are welcomed with a simple reminder: there's no turning back.

and open staircases twist and turn throughout the structure, taking visitors on a vertical journey. From the arrival of the grain to the spirits' transformation, the journey continues up multiple levels where the final product greets guests at the end of the journey.

Once the tour ends, innovative cocktails and cuisine from Rabbit Hole's master chef and mixologists await guests on the upper level. Outfitted with a bar, restaurant, and overlook, the atmosphere is hip and cool and you can't help but want to be a part of it. And the views of the city are fabulous.

"We wanted to create a place where transparency is more than a marketing slogan," he said. "This showcases art and science, and allows visitors to be mesmerized in it."

Nowhere is that more evident than in the massive atrium anchored by nine 8,000-gallon fermenters and continuous

#breatheairdrinkbourbon

The clean lines of metal, wood, and concrete on one of the exterior passageways at Rabbit Hole Distillery reflect the influence of Ludwig Mies van der Rohe, one of the pioneers of modernist architecture.

column copper still that rises more than forty-six feet in the air. The result is a magical, if not spiritual, feeling of being in a cathedral, which is exactly what Kaveh had hoped for.

"I felt like it was time for someone to push the envelope," he said. "We want to evoke a sense of curiosity, to get people excited, and elevate (bourbon) to the next level."

Makes perfect sense to me. This is Rabbit Hole Distillery after all, and there's no turning back. But why would anyone want to?

Rabbit Hole is located at 711 East Jefferson Street, in Louisville, Kentucky. For more information, check out the website at rabbitholedistillery.com, email info@rabbitholedistillery.com or call 502.561-2000.

According to a new study, drinking whiskey prolongs your life.

Looks like I'm gonna be immortal.

Rabbit Hole Distillery Visit

Notes:

These two recipes come from Chris Wilkins, Rabbit Hole Distillery's marketing manager and brand representative. Thanks for sharing, Chris!

Air Kentucky

¾ oz. Rabbit Hole Bourbon
¾ oz. Rammazzotti Amaro
¾ oz. Aperol
¾ oz. Lemon juice

Combine ingredients in a mixing tin. Add ice. Shake thoroughly. Fine strain into a coupe or martini glass and enjoy.
*(This is a riff on a classic bourbon cocktail: Paper Plane.)

Double Gold Rush

1 ½ oz. Rabbit Hole Bourbon
¾ oz. Apple-Honey syrup
¾ oz. Lemon juice

Combine ingredients in a mixing tin. Add ice. Shake thoroughly. Strain in to a double Old Fashioned glass. Fill with ice. Garnish with a lemon peel.

*Apple- Honey Syrup
Slice a Golden Delicious apple in to thin slices. In a pot, heat 8 oz. of water to a simmer. Add 8 oz. of raw honey and stir frequently. Once honey is fully incorporated, add apple slices. Let simmer for 30 minutes. Make sure not to boil. When finished, strain and let cool.

TO BARDSTOWN BY WAY OF ST. LOUIS

You may not know it, but I'm betting you're familiar with Luxco, the St. Louis-based spirits company and producers of vodka, gin, tequila and other spirits. It's also behind such names as Ezra Brooks, Rebel Yell, and David Nicholson's 1843. You also may not know that until the last couple of years, Luxco relied on others to produce their bourbons.

In 2016, Luxco took its future in its hands and broke ground on an 18,000-square-foot facility in Bardstown. In the spring of 2018, the corporation opened Lux Row Distillers, with the capacity to distill three million gallons of whiskey a year.

Donn Lux, Chairman & CEO of Luxco (the parent to Lux Row Distillers) and his wife, Michele Lux (Lux Row Creative Director) have been hands-on from the distillery's inception.

Michael Cooley, retail manager, hopes visitors to Lux Row feel like they're stopping by to see an old friend.

From the distillery's name — an ode to the rows of barrels, rows of grain, rows of bottles, and rows of trees that line the winding drive from the main road to the distillery — to light fixtures and aviator chairs in the gift shop, chosen to illustrate her husband's love of flying — Michele's personal touches can be seen in a variety of elements throughout the property.

Lux Row Distillers retail manager Michael Cooley said their goal is two-fold: to make good whiskey and provide a friendly, welcoming experience for visitors — a personal touch that feels like home.

"To be part of this from the beginning and getting to work with Michele to bring her vision to life has been amazing," the retail manager said. "Bottom line, all of us at Lux Row hope every visit feels like dropping by to see an old friend. We serve the same chocolate Michele and Donn have been serving in their own home for years. That's the vibe we want to create here, an extension of the family home."

For more information, visit luxrowdistillers.com

Lux Row Distillery Visit

Notes:

THE SPIRITS MADE BY GHOSTS

Bourbon legacies are often handed down from one generation to the next, as sons, and nephews, grandsons, and great-grandsons carry on the traditions of those who came before them.

Sometimes though, history must be discovered—reclaimed along the way. Saved from certain annihilation, if you will.

Such is the case at Boone County Distilling Company, where they're breathing new life into a story that had been all but forgotten. It's a story that begins in 1833 — and one to which they're proud to trace their roots.

The year of 1833 was the birth year of such notables as future U.S. president Benjamin Harrison, composer Johannes Brahms (yes, the lullaby guy), and the notorious Samuel Mudd (the physician accused of co-conspiring Abraham Lincoln's death). It was also the year that brothers William and John Snyder purchased the Petersburg Steam Mill in Petersburg, Kentucky, and within three years started the Petersburg Distillery alongside of that, but was later known as the Boone County Distillery.

"This was the time when distilling was coming out of the backwoods and becoming part of everyday industry," said distillery worker Michael Thornton.

Distillery worker Michael Thornton, who is also a wonderful photographer, loves to tell the stories behind Boone County Distilling. As it turns out, his family tree can be traced back to the same parts of Virginia as the Snyders and Loders.

Photo courtesy Boone County Distillery

By the end of the nineteenth century, workers at Petersburg Distillery were producing four million gallons of whiskey per year.

Although the owners changed over the course of the next sixty-some years, the distillery, which also included a mill and livestock complex, brought a hub of activity and prominence to the river town.

By 1860, at a time when the cost of corn was twenty-five cents a bushel and a gallon of whiskey nearly a dollar, Petersburg Distillery was producing more than one million gallons of whiskey a year. Not too shabby at all. But production at the distillery was just starting to hit its stride. At its zenith in 1897, it was the second largest distillery in the nation, producing over four million gallons of whiskey a year.

Unbeknownst to many, some major changes were afoot in the world of distilling as a number of whiskey trusts were formed in an effort to monopolize the industry. Kentucky

Distilleries and Warehouse Company was among them. Its intentions were simple: to acquire and shutter distilleries in an effort to reduce competition. Petersburg Distillery — Registered Distillery Plant # 8 — was among the casualties.

Coupled with the decline in steamboat travel and increase in rail transportation, the distillery's closure accelerated the demise of an entire town, most especially those who had carved out their livelihoods at the distillery.

By the end of 1918 little remained. As the years moved on, the distillery — and its impact on the community it once called home — faded into near oblivion.

Almost a hundred years would pass before longtime friends Josh Quinn and Jack Wells bandied about the idea of building a distillery in Northern Kentucky. As their plans took root, the Petersburg Distillery was reclaimed, piece by piece.

A longtime Boone County resident, Josh Quinn wanted to save and share some of the rich history of the industry and the area.

Today, a new Boone County Distilling Company is reconnecting area residents with a past that had been forgotten in some cases, unrealized in others. Visits to the distillery often segue to a genealogy session — even for Thornton, whose family came from the same part of Virginia as the Snyders and Louis Loder.

"We're honoring the ghosts of those original distillery workers who paved the way for us," Thornton said. "If not for them, we wouldn't be here today."

The Loder Diaries

Much of the distillery and Boone County history was recorded by Lewis Loder, who worked for William Snyder as a bookkeeper. Loder's diary entries, relating fifty-seven years of history, recall distillery life, and life in Kentucky in the mid to late 1800s. He even wrote about the total eclipse of the sun on August 7, 1869.

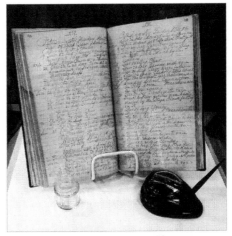

Photo courtesy of Boone County Distillery

Some of his most entertaining entries referred to his boss, who happened to own a bear.

Lewis Loder kept this diary for more than fifty years.

Here's an entry from Loder's diary, dated August 21, 1857:

> *"Mr Snyder's Bear got loose & Bit a Girl and run half over the Town But he Jumpt over into Mrs Snelling's yard and Perry McNeely caught him they tied a large cable to the Piece of chain that was to him & took him back to his box."*

Want to read more of Loder's diary entries? Follow @madebyghosts on Twitter.

The story of Tanner's Curse

One of the products available at Boone County Distilling is Tanner's Curse.

"Tanner's Curse honors the region's rather wild and tumultuous history," Thornton said.

Available in a new make rye mash and a new make bourbon mash whiskey, one needn't look further than the label to know there's got to be a good story behind the curse.

And indeed there is. Here's a nutshell version to hold you over. And when you visit, be sure to have the fine folks at Boone County Distilling fill in all the gory details.

Photo courtesy of Boone County Distillery

Tanner's Curse is a prime example of how *not* to practice hospitality.

It seems Reverend John Tanner was a Baptist circuit rider in the late 1700s. He traveled on horseback from one settlement to another, bringing religion to those who needed it, and hightailing it away from those who didn't.

In 1791, he decided it was time to put down some roots, so he established Tanner's Station along the banks of the Ohio River — the first settlement in Boone County, Kentucky.

So far, so good, right?

Wrong.

Unfortunately, Tanner built on the massive burial grounds of Fort Ancient Indians, igniting a series of fateful events that sent Tanner and his family on a downward spiral of doom in the years that followed.

One son was scalped by Indians, another ripped apart by wild hogs. A third son was captured by Shawnee Indians while picking walnuts from his favorite tree. If that's not the workings of a curse, I don't know what is.

Boone County Distilling is located about fifteen miles south of Cincinnati, less than two miles off I-75, Exit 178. For additional information including tours, visit their website at boonedistilling.com.

Boone County Distillery Visit

Notes:
_____

Bourbon Cream Chocolate Martini

Courtesy of Boone County Distilling

From topping off coffee to making whipped cream and cheesecakes, bourbon cream is a top contender for after-dinner drinks, desserts, and around-the-clock deliciousness. If you've never tried it, here's a recipe from Boone County Distilling that'll have you tracking down a bottle ASAP.

Ingredients

4 oz Bourbon Cream
½ oz. Boone County's Bourbon
½ oz. Cream de Cocoa
¼ oz. Coffee Liqueur

Directions

Swirl martini glass with chocolate syrup, shake all ingredients together with ice to chill, pour and enjoy.

A STORY OF MOONSHINE

To say that Royce Neeley's introduction into the world of distilling was unconventional is an understatement. He was attending a fraternity party at a Lexington, Kentucky, university where he ran into a former classmate who was selling an ever-clear based concoction he was calling "Moonshine" for twenty-five dollars a gallon — and the students he was selling it to did not realize this guy was a fraud.

"I immediately recognized an opportunity," Royce said. "I knew about my family's moonshining stories and our family recipe, but didn't really know much about running my own operation."

#moonshineisfine

Royce Neeley makes his spirits with a sweet mash, following in the footsteps of his great-grandfather.

He knew moonshining in the Neeley family had a long history, dating back eleven generations to 1740, with ancestors who'd made their way from Ireland to Owsley County, in Eastern Kentucky. So Royce approached his father and uncles to see what they could tell him. They told Royce everything he wanted to know. What they didn't realize was he was putting the knowledge into practical application.

Once he had a basic understanding of the process, the chemical and business major went to work on building his own still, which he kept in his Lexington house. With the help of his roommates, he was soon distilling through the week while he studied, and selling on the weekends.

Photo courtesy of Royce Neeley

"Since I was distilling my own shine, I could sell mine for ten dollars less a gallon, and it tasted a whole lot better," he said.

Royce Neeley still adds wild yeast from the family farm in Owsley County to his mash. His methods of collection include a five-gallon bucket.

"Once I got a taste for it, I just couldn't stop doing it. I loved distilling and seeing people's reactions to it. Everybody loved it. It was definitely in my blood."

His lower price, coupled with a better tasting product, gave him an upper hand on the black market of moonshining, and his former classmate was the first person he put out of business.

Word of Royce's new venture spread quickly. In the world of illegal moonshining though, popularity can be a blessing and a curse. Royce knew he needed to get the still out of Lexington. He also knew he needed to make a change. He needed to distill legally.

"There were several times I thought I'd get caught. I always had to stay a step or two ahead," he said. "I soon figured out I wanted to get it legal. I wanted to experiment and start manipulating the mash bills. I wanted to take my family name from the mountains of Eastern Kentucky to the Kentucky Bourbon Trail."

With his decision made, he shut down the still, vowing not to make anything else illegally.

"From that day on, I've been completely legal. We do everything strictly by the law," Royce said.

The distilling bug had already consumed him, so he did a lot of research, crunched a few numbers, found some property in Sparta, Kentucky, and approached his dad with a business plan. Aside from making the best product he was capable of producing, he also wanted to make sure that building and running the distillery would be a completely family-funded venture. Thanks to both his parents' business know-how and successful past business ventures, Royce's dream became a reality.

"I knew if we couldn't do it ourselves and make it on our own, then it wasn't worth doing," he said. "That was April of 2015. Thirty-two days later, Mom, Dad, and I bought the property, and I have been working seven days a week, three-hundred-sixty-five days a year since."

Today, he uses his great grandfather's original "sweet mash" recipe that calls for Domino® Cane Sugar among its ingredients — Royce says that's why his mash is so good. He also follows a triple pot distilling method, like his forefathers.

"We focus on being authentic — we're quality driven, not quantity driven, doing things the old way," he said. "We let Mother Nature take her course. It's not always the easiest way, but it is the best way."

To that end, he still adds wild yeast to every product he makes. He gathers it from the family property in Owsley

Photo courtesy of Royce Neeley

Royce Neeley, left, and Earl "Papa" Sizemore.

County with a five-gallon "dona" jug and cheesecloth, and propagates it inside his distillery.

"We're moonshiners making some of Kentucky's best bourbon," he said, noting that by the fall of 2018, they had 300 barrels aging with more to come.

Equally as important is remembering where he came from. "We're always gonna be making moonshine and using pot stills."

Legally, of course.

113

All in the Family

Running the Neeley Family Distillery is a true family affair. Roy Neeley does all the building and construction (and helps run the stills), while his wife Michele takes care of the storefront. She's the mastermind behind the cocktails, which feature the seven moonshines they're producing, and she also coordinates distillery events.

Royce's maternal grandfather, Earl "Papa" Sizemore, gets the stills going at six o'clock each morning. And when Royce is out and about, chances are good Papa is with him.

Moonshining Lineage

When it comes to family stories passed down through multiple generations, Royce acknowledged it can be tough to know what to believe.

"Sometimes you wonder what's true and what's not," he said.

But once family in Eastern Kentucky learned about Royce's new venture, they started sending him articles and clippings from newspapers over 100 years old, verifying what he'd been told over the years. In addition to confirming the family lineage for moonshining and bootlegging, the clippings also confirmed life for moonshiners was anything but easy. Royce's great-grandfather's still had been in hiding since the 1970s by family members deep in the mountains. It is on display in the gift shop and is still functioning.

"It was life or death for them," he said. "But it beat working in the coal mines."

Royce's dad, Roy, observed many of those stories. Most days, he can be found at the distillery, so when you visit, be sure to track him down and ask him about the pistol in the display case — or the rifle with eight notches in it.

Neeley Family Distillery is located at 4360 KY 1130 in Sparta, Kentucky, right up from Kentucky Speedway. For more information, call 859-394-3258 or visit t heir Facebook page @neeleyfamilydistillery.

Neeley Family Distillery Visit

Notes:

_____

_____

_____

_____

_____

_____

_____

_____

_____

_____

_____

_____

_____

Slow Cooker Bourbon Kielbasa

INGREDIENTS:

1 pound Kielbasa, sliced
1 cup apricot preserves
½ cup maple syrup
2 T. bourbon or apple juice

DIRECTIONS:

Combine all in a crockpot, cover and cook on low for four hours.

AN URBAN RIFF ON AN OLD TRADITION

I love a good story about grit, ingenuity, and success. And if you're a bourbon fan, you know the industry is no stranger to these stories. Many a keen mind, business acumen and adventurous spirit can be found within it.

Ken Lewis is a prime example of that. A self-made man, Ken has worked in the beverage and alcohol industry for more than three decades. It was plenty of time to build up a dynasty in the liquor arena, which incidentally, was exactly what he did.

At twenty-four, he took over his uncle's liquor store in Louisville. By the time he was forty, the native Kentuckian owned six Liquor Outlet/Party Source stores doing over 65 million dollars in annual sales, employed 350 people, and was far and away the dominant beverage alcohol retailer in Kentucky.

Ken Lewis is an entrepreneur at heart. While he honors the men and women of the bourbon world who've come before him, he's doing things his own way.

Sometimes, though, success can get in the way of happiness, and all work and no play left Ken looking for a better way forward. To that end, he sold all but one of the Party Source stores to Liquor Barn in 2010, and devoted his time to the remaining location in Newport, Kentucky. For those of you wondering, and for purposes of reference, that store remains the largest beverage alcohol store in the nation.

I'm guessing I don't have to tell you his financial situation was such that he could've spent the second half of his life sipping cocktails and counting people on the iconic Purple People Bridge, the pedestrian bridge connecting the cities of Newport, Kentucky, and Cincinnati, Ohio.

Had he chosen that route, I suspect boredom would've over come him in about three seconds flat. Adventurous spirits de-test boredom.

Instead, he followed a hunch.

"I'm a risk-taker — an entrepreneur at heart," Lewis said. "I saw a dramatic bourbon boom happening in front of me."

He also recognized opportunity and explored his options.

Two realities occurred to him. Nearly every distillery in the state was taking a pastoral approach to making bourbon, and none of them were doing so in Northern Kentucky or Cincinnati.

"There was room for an urban approach," Ken said. And from that realization, New Riff Distilling was born. "I wasn't in it to change the bourbon world. What I wanted was to interpret it in my own way, to put my own slant on it."

First though, he'd have to sell his remaining Party Source store — the nation's three-tier alcohol system prohibits a single entity from manufacturing, retailing, and distributing. Instead of selling to a corporation, Ken sold the store to his employees.

"Sure, it meant more hoops to jump through and maybe wasn't the very top dollar return, but for me it was absolutely the right thing to do."

He retained ownership of the land the Party Source occupies, though, and had plenty of space to build a distillery

New Riff Distillery is located adjacent to The Party Source in Newport, Kentucky.

on site. All he had to do was move a massive flood wall. But what's a million-dollar flood wall when there's bourbon to be made?

As plans for the distillery continued to materialize, he brought in master distiller Larry Ebersold, the just-retired master distiller for Seagrams (now Midwest Grain Products, or MGP, in Lawrenceburg, Indiana.) The addition of Ebersold, who is renowned as the inventor of the 95/5 rye whiskey recipe, was a harbinger for things to come. As was the decision to bring in former beer brewer Brian Sprance as head distiller.

"Brewers understand fermentation," Ken said. "You've got to start with good fermentation."

Additional team players came on board while construction simultaneously continued on the new 30,000-foot facility, which opened to the public in 2014. With two event spaces, views of the city, and a 24-inch Vendome copper column still, rising sixty feet into the air as a focal point, New

Nice try, diamonds. But we all know who a girl's real best friend is. Sincerely, Bourbon

Riff assumed the role of host to a variety of events, from corporate meetings to weddings.

If there was an immediate problem, it was bourbon — or lack thereof. New Riff Distillery bourbon had four years left to age. Not because of external mandates — there are no rules governing the amount of time bourbon must age — but because of a self-imposed mandate Ken established early on.

"We are all about quality and knew we wanted to wait four plus years and bring our whiskey to market exclusively as Bottled in Bond or Barrel Proof and without chill filtration."

That said, Ken knew visitors would want to sample a product after touring the distillery, so he sourced a high rye bourbon — one in keeping with what he expected from his own product. Bottled as O.K.I., the name was a nod to Ohio, Kentucky and Indiana, the golden geographic triangle where New Riff is located.

It proved the perfect stopgap measure that harmonized with Ken's long-term goals.

"At some point, the bubble will burst," he said, referring to market saturation. "Our approach is that it's already happened."

It's an attitude that pairs well with the waiting game — not to mention that deep down inside, we all know a little anticipation is good for the soul. And that brings us four years forward to the summer of 2018, and the release of New Riff Kentucky Straight Bourbon Whiskey.

The wait was rewarded on the Purple People Bridge, where 2,200 bourbon and tourism fans gathered for the #BigBourbonToast that spanned two states no doubt an official declaration to the world that New Riff would be putting their own riff on everything they produce.

"Our mission is to be one of the great small distilleries in the world," Ken said. "We appreciate the tradition of Kentucky

Photo courtesy of New Riff Distillery

The Big Bourbon Toast, hosted by New Riff Distillery spanned two states and attracted roughly 2,200 bourbon and tourism fans.

TALK BOURBON TO ME! 2

bourbon, and there's some wonderful whiskey being made. But we're doing our own guitar riff. Writing our own song."

From the looks and taste of things, it'll soon be a song any bourbon or rye whiskey fan will know by heart.

Rye-centric Future

As any musician knows, a good riff balances creativity and skill. As Ken will tell you, a good riff also means trusting your instincts to create a unique vibe.

"I didn't set out to do it," he said, "but the distillery is telling me it wants to be a rye distillery."

While some may raise an eyebrow at the notion of a living, breathing distillery calling the shots, Ken's gut tells him rye is the way forward.

"I feel it fits us, and it's something that's quickly becoming a focal point," he said. "I think we're going to have a phenomenal reputation as a rye distillery."

To that end, New Riff Distillery's 100 Percent Rye (95 rye/malted rye) should be out by early winter 2018. By all indications, both distillery and distiller know exactly what they're talking about.

Discovering the Aquifer

When construction began on New Riff Distillery, Ken Lewis planned to do what all the other distilleries do — bring in water from the city and purchase massive chillers to cool it down for distilling purposes.

"Someone mentioned to us that there used to be a lot of wells in the Newport area," he said. And sure enough, they discovered an alluvial aquifer under the distillery, 100 feet below the surface.

Their first order of business was to conduct a full lab analysis. When all was said and done, the analysis confirmed they were sitting on the perfect hard water for distilling, flowing at a rate of 500 gallons per minute.

"It's fifty-eight degrees year round (eliminating the need for a chiller), it comes out fresh with no processing, and it's rich in calcium and minerals."

In other words, it's water that's begging to become whiskey.

Three-Tier System of Alcohol Distribution

As I wrote earlier, once Ken decided to enter the distilling arena, he was legally bound to make an exit from the retail level. Why? After the repeal of Prohibition, the U.S. Government established a three-tier system for alcohol distribution:

* Producers (distillers and brewers)
* Distributors
* Retailers

While laws in each state vary considerably, the tiers provide walls of separation to prevent any one entity from gaining too much power in the industry — which is part of what led to Prohibition in the first place.

In Kentucky, an individual or business who produces alcohol as a business can't also distribute or sell alcohol in another business. They must choose one. Take that, Al Capone.

New Riff West Campus

Once home to the Green Line trolley and bus system, New Riff's second whiskey campus — the west campus — is a unique blend of past and present.

The older buildings, built in the last few years of the nineteenth century, house the bottling area and part of New Riff's aging space, while a

What was once part of the Green Line trolley and bus system, is now used to bottle and age New Riff bourbon.

new 300-by-65-foot rick house, five ricks high, offers additional space for eighteen thousand barrels.

Located a couple of miles from the distillery, the west campus location also includes office space, a gift shop, tasting room, and additional storage.

Amy Tobin, director of communications, said the west campus serves as a reminder of how far they've come in these last few years. She recalled one winter early in New Riff's existence, when all employees, numbering less than a dozen at that point, worked to count the barrels in one of the older buildings.

"We were counting barrels in full winter garb, Carhart coveralls, the works," she said. "A couple of the petite women who could squeeze in between the barrels were literally scampering over them, sometimes hanging off or sandwiched in between barrels to stick on stickers and count barrels."

While their manual barrel-counting days are behind them, she says they realized even then that the day would be significant on down the line.

The Hidden Room

The building that houses tastings, bottling, offices, and a small gift shop at the west campus location was built in 1896. During the renovation process, Amy recalled walking through the building with the architect, when she noticed a round opening covered in plywood, behind a stack of barrels.

Photo courtesy of New Riff Distilling

Among other activities, New Riff's West Campus is where the bottling and aging happen. Specialty tours are also available on site.

Photo courtesy of New Riff Distilling

What was once a hidden room at the west campus offers an historic feel to the New Riff experience, meshing history with the present.

"We're climbing up on the barrels, shining our cell phone lights in the cracks of the plywood, and I remember saying, 'Oh my God, there's a room in there!'

"We saw it as a chance to create a very special room —an opportunity to really make a statement." Amy said.

Fire Suppression

To say bourbon is highly flammable is an understatement. In fact, the traditional reaction in case of fire can be summed up in one word: Run!

That scenario isn't an option as far as New Riff is concerned. It can't be. Unlike a pastoral distillery, New Riff is in the middle of a neighborhood.

> "No matter what we do, it always comes back to a sense of how you do one thing is how you do everything."
>
> —Amy Tobin, New Riff Director of Communications.

To that end, they've installed the same fire suppression system that's used by CVG (Cincinnati/Northern Kentucky International) Airport.

"Our system is capable of putting out a jet airliner, and when our local departments trained for our system, they did so at CVG," Amy said. "I think that gives an idea of how serious we are about protecting the community."

New Riff Distilling is located in Newport, Kentucky. For additional information, or to book a tour or tasting, visit their website at newriffdistilling.com.

New Riff Distillery Visit

Notes:

Bourbon Butter Pretzels

INGREDIENTS

2 bags of pretzels (I use the small twists or sticks)
1 stick butter
3 T bourbon
1 T brown sugar, heaping
½ t. of cayenne pepper
1 t. garlic powder
1-2 baking sheets, lined with parchment paper

DIRECTIONS

Preheat oven to 250 degrees. Pour pretzels into large mixing bowl. In a medium saucepan, melt butter and add whiskey, brown sugar, pepper and garlic powder. Stir until well combined. Pour over pretzels. Be sure to stir well to coat all the pretzels. Spread onto baking sheets, and bake 20-30 minutes. Allow to cool, then store in an airtight container.

Infinity Bottles

Have you ever mixed cola and orange soda, root beer and lemon lime, or all of the above? When I was young, we did it all the time.

Believe it or not, people are doing the same type of thing with their distilled spirits these days. And they refer to the mix as an infinity bottle. It makes sense — when I look around at my bottles, more than a few have only a pour or two left. By making my own Infinity Bottle, I could not only make space for new bottles, I could also conduct my own bourbon experiments, crude as they might be. Regardless, it's an idea I'm willing to try. Here's how it's done.

Infinity Bottles can be just about anything you want them to be. You could keep a bottle for bourbons and one for gin, another for Tennessee whiskey and so on. Or you can make a crazy mix of all the above.

From what I can gather, there aren't any hard and fast rules, unless you drink peated whiskeys — in which case you're advised to tread lightly if at all. You can use an old bottle you've been saving, or purchase something special to use for this purpose. Add a label and you'll be able to keep track of what you've poured into your bottle. Let me know if you try it. We'll compare notes.

ON THE ROAD IN BOURBON COUNTRY

One of the most stress-free ways to explore Bourbon Country is to enlist the services of others, particularly those who specialize in tours. We've got a variety of tour providers to choose from here in the Commonwealth, and I must say, it sounds like a job I'd love to have. I wanted to know more about life on the road for those who offer tours, so I caught up with Tim Hagan, acting as official spokesman of the Kentucky Bourbon Boys. Here's a look at what they had to say.

Talk Bourbon: *What's the Kentucky Bourbon Boys all about?*

Kentucky Bourbon Boys: The Kentucky Bourbon Boys business grew out of a social organization formed in 2011. We

Photo courtesy of the Kentucky Bourbon Boys

The guys (and gal) at Kentucky Bourbon Boys can trace their family roots back to 1780s Bardstown.

offer private and customized tours only, and we pick up groups wherever they want. One of our most memorable visitors flew his plane into the Georgetown airport, and our van went out to the plane to unload their luggage, and head out on the bourbon trail. We do aim to please. We formed our business as a family operation, and we all still get along nicely.

Talk Bourbon: *Do you guys have family connections to the bourbon industry?*

Kentucky Bourbon Boys: One thing you should know is our family has early roots in Kentucky (the 1780s) and of course were among the group of Catholic families that settled in the Bardstown area, coming from Maryland. Hagan, Thompson,

Mattingly, and Dant were all settled around St. Francis, which was called "Chicago" at some point, Loretto, and New Hope, Kentucky. J.W. Dant was the brother of my mother's great-great-grandfather. There is nothing left of his distillery now — but there is a road sign labeled "Dant Station" just west of St. Francis. And J.W. Dant is buried behind the church there.

Talk Bourbon: *Who are some of the must-meet people for those visiting Bourbon Country?*

Kentucky Bourbon Boys:

Some must-meet folks work at every distillery, but some who stand out for our guests include Steve Fante at Limestone Branch. Just meet him and nothing else has to be said. When visiting the Bulleit Experience at Stitzel-Weller, it's hard to avoid telling guests to skip the tour and go hang out with Carroll Perry at the welcome building. If you are at Buffalo Trace, so many guides are so good it's impossible to recommend one, but we always enjoy getting to see Freddie Johnson, whose

Ask anyone who's met Limestone Branch's Steve Fante, and they'll tell you his personality is larger than life. A born entertainer and a barrel of fun, he also knows a thing or two about bourbon.

story is inspiring and entertaining.

When we visit Wild Turkey, it's difficult to describe the joy on the faces of our guests when they see Jimmy and Joretta Russell hanging out in the visitors center. Jimmy and Joretta happily pose for pictures and sign bottles, tell stories, and show interest in everyone they meet.

Talk Bourbon: *I've noticed some of the other entertaining tour guides are four-legged felines.*

Kentucky Bourbon Boys: Yes, there are lots of distillery cats out there — and it's difficult to remember all their names. I know at Willett you'll see Noah and Rowan wandering along with the visitors, or lounging in the visitors center. At Jeptha Creed, you can visit with Malt, Rye, Wheat, and Barley. At Maker's you'll see Whisky Jean hanging out at the house —

Photo courtesy of Barrel House Distillery

Snuggy, one of the distillery cats at Barrel House Distilling, stands off against a crawfish at the distillery's tenth anniversary celebration. He enjoys socializing with guests, so stop by and meet at 1200 Manchester Street in Lexington.

usually waiting for someone to open the door to go inside or out.

Talk Bourbon: *Do you run into many celebrities?*

Kentucky Bourbon Boys: You never know who you'll see out on the trail — lots of celebrities come these days, and some who might be known only within a certain niche. We ran into Jason Smith, winner of "Next Food Network Star" at Wallace Station in Midway.

Most people may not know him, but we toured with Rob Peterson and his family. Rob carves trees into beautiful sculptures around Kentucky (you can see his work at Springdale Presbyterian Church, on Watterson Trail, and near

Photo courtesy of the Kentucky Bourbon Boys

Rob Peterson is a local artist whose work appears at various locations in Kentucky, including Barton's 1792 Distillery in Bardstown.

Photo courtesy of the Kentucky Bourbon Boys
Each October, the Kentucky Bourbon Boys hold a guys-only event they call "Bullets and Bourbon", which includes chili and plenty of bourbon, of course.

Holiday Manor), and we visited his work at Barton's.

Talk Bourbon: *Do you host any special events throughout the year?*

Kentucky Bourbon Boys: Each year, we hold several outings and invite members to come out and enjoy a visit to a new distillery, have lunch together, or participate in other activities. A "guys only" event each October has become a favorite — we gather on a family farm for "Bullets and Bourbon" where we shoot all day, enjoy chili for dinner, and have a bourbon tasting. Up to twenty participants over the years have allowed for tasting over a hundred bourbons, declaring a winner each year. And no worries, there is a competition to see how many "Mr. Safety" directors we can have on site so we can enjoy our day without incident.

Talk Bourbon: *What's your favorite part about offering bourbon tours?*

Kentucky Bourbon Boys: We see clients come as guests, and leave as friends. We love sharing our old Kentucky home with visitors, and see it as a mission to present Kentucky in all its beauty, history, and culture. Our tours have seen guests from all over the country, and we're seeing a rapid increase in visitors from overseas. We often see guests pulling up Zillow on their phones and checking the price of land and homes in the area, and we have great conversations about all the things Kentucky has to offer. So far, we've made a lot of new friends.

Photo courtesy of Breaking Bourbon

The Bourbon Heritage Center at Heaven Hill Distillery is always a great place to visit in Bardstown.

Bourbon and Bacon Party Mix

This is always a crowd favorite. I often have it on hand for book signings and it disappears every time.

INGREDIENTS

1 15 oz. bag Chex Mix traditional snack mix
1 cup pecan halves
½ lb. bacon (6-8 slices), cooked crisp and crumbled
½ cup packed brown sugar
½ cup butter
¼ cup light corn syrup
2 T. bourbon
¾ t. chipotle chili powder

DIRECTIONS

Heat oven to 300 degrees. Line two sheet pans with foil, and spray with cooking spray. In a large bowl, mix snack mix, pecans, and bacon. Set aside.

In 2-quart saucepan, heat brown sugar, butter, and corn syrup over medium heat, stirring occasionally until bubbly around edges. Cook 5 minutes, stirring occasionally. And remove from heat. Cool 2 minutes. Carefully stir in bourbon and chipotle chili powder. Pour over snack mixture and toss until evenly coated.

Spread snack mixture on pans. Bake 15 minutes, stirring every 5 minutes, to caramelize mix. Cool completely, about an hour. Break into pieces, and store in refrigerator.

Note: Can be stored in an airtight container at room temperature if you omit the bacon, or add just before serving.

EVER DRANK SO MUCH BOURBON THAT YOU WOKE UP THE NEXT MORNING WITH A KENTUCKY ACCENT?

BETH UNDERWOOD

PASSING THE BATON

Before we close the cover on *Talk Bourbon to Me 2*, I've got one more story I want to share with you — a personal story that unfolded as I explored the grounds of Buffalo Trace Distillery with Freddie Johnson. As many of you may know, Freddie is the distillery's VIP Visitor Lead, a member of the Kentucky Bourbon Hall of Fame, and an icon in his own right.

On this particular day, in between official bourbon banter, climbing over a couple of walls, and stopping for photos, our conversations turned to his years at the distillery, and how it had come to pass.

A third-generation employee, Freddie follows in the footsteps of his father, Jimmy Jr., and grandfather, Jimmy Sr., and still remembers playing on the grounds of the distillery when he was five years old. Unlike his father and grandfather, though, he didn't immediately embrace the idea of working in the industry. In fact, when he graduated from school, the bourbon industry was dead, which was fine with Freddie —

Freddie Johnson, VIP Visitor Lead at Buffalo Trace Distillery in Frankfort, Kentucky, started working at the distillery to make good on a promise he made to his father. Seventeen years later, you can still find him there most every day — except for Thursdays.

much of Freddie's adult life was spent as a network operations manager and engineer for AT&T.

But he'd made two promises to his dad early on.

"We made an agreement that if (bourbon) ever came back, I'd work at the distillery — give it a try for one year. And I promised to be his caregiver if anything ever happened to him," Freddie said. "These old guys can ask in such a way as to massage you into a pit of doom."

In 2000, a mid-afternoon phone call changed the course of Freddie's life.

"It was Dad. He said, 'The good news is I love you. The bad news is I'm terminally ill.'"

As fate would orchestrate, Freddie was about to make good on both promises. Initially, he continued working for AT&T and traveled to Frankfort one day a week.

"I'd always go to chemo treatments with him on Thursdays. One trip in, I stayed the whole weekend," Freddie said. "I didn't know Dad was so sick. All of a sudden, I see it, and I was broken-hearted."

Soon after, Freddie took early retirement from AT&T, while Jimmy Johnson continued to go to the distillery any day he was well enough to go, making sure his son accompanied him.

"Looking back, he was handing off the baton. 'Don't forget this. Remember that,' he'd say."

For a moment, Freddie was silent, allowing those memories to replay in his mind. As he continued, I began to wonder what was in that figurative baton passed from father to son.

Certainly it held a wealth of bourbon knowledge — no one knows the history at Buffalo Trace better than Freddie. And no doubt it held all the ingredients needed to tell a good story — no one weaves a better story than Freddie.

It held the keys to a family's strength and loyalty — the distillery grounds that saw his grandfather making whiskey during Prohibition saw his father roll out the distillery's six-millionth barrel in 2008, and watched Freddie and his grandson, Osiris Johnson roll out the seven-millionth barrel in 2018.

But there was something more — something else in that baton was eluding me.

As our time together continued, we made our way to the second floor of the visitor center, and headed to the bar to enjoy some hooch as Freddie endearingly refers to it.

Photo courtesy of Buffalo Trace Distillery

Freddie Johnson and his grandson, Osiris Johnson, roll out the seven millionth barrel of bourbon on April 12, 2018.

He told me how his attitude had changed through the years, noting he use to believe there was a right and wrong way to drink bourbon — and he wasn't afraid to set someone straight if they were doing it wrong.

He'd loosened up considerably through the years, though, evidenced by the story he told me next.

One night in particular, Freddie was spending the evening with his brother and dad. Freddie's dad brought out a bottle of Pappy Van Winkle, which had been given to him by Julian Van Winkle.

"I wanted to save that bottle," Freddie said. "But Dad said, 'I'm 94-years-old, son. I don't have a lot of toasting left.'"

Freddie relinquished three pours and re-corked the bottle, hoping to save the rest.

But his father had other ideas.

"He said, 'There will always be more whiskey, son. We're the delicate piece in this whole thing. It's far better to make the memories, because we won't always be here to do it.'"

The three men went on to enjoy the best conversations of their lives that evening. And by the end of the night, the bottle was empty. Within nine months of that night, both Freddie's father and brother passed away.

"That night changed my life," Freddie said.

Since that night, Freddie has continued to share his days — and his stories — with visitors to Buffalo Trace Distillery. His promise to work there for one year has extended into seventeen. He still doesn't work on Thursdays, though. And he's no longer worried about saving that special bottle for another time.

"Grab that special bottle of hooch. Go ahead and share it with someone you love and make a few memories and start your own traditions," Freddie said. "Sure, we all love the bourbon. But it's those long-term relationships that are most important. The bourbon will outlive us all."

And that's when it occurred to me. The baton has been a part of bourbon since the beginning. It was the impetus behind everything Colonel Taylor and the other forefathers of bourbon hoped to accomplish more than a hundred years ago. It is the driving force behind every proud distillery worker here in Bourbon Country. And it's that special voice that calls to us with every bottle of bourbon we enjoy.

It's the spirit of hospitality.

THE END

Enjoy this book? You can make a big difference.

Reviews are one of the most powerful marketing tools an author has, and honest reviews can help bring this book to the attention of other bourbon fans.

If you've enjoyed this book, found it entertaining, informative, or otherwise useful in your pursuit of all things bourbon, I would be grateful if you'd consider leaving a short review on the book's Amazon page. Thank you.

Other books by Beth Underwood:

Talk Bourbon to Me: A whiskey lover's guide to Kentucky's favorite spirit (2016)

The first in the series, *Talk Bourbon to Me* takes a look at the whiskey long revered by Kentuckians and the world at large. This one-of-a-kind spirit makes our bluegrass bluer, our basketball wins sweeter, and our horses faster.

Talk Bourbon to Me brings readers the step-by-step age-old process for practical distilling as it was done in the early 1800s, then brings things into the twenty-first century with up-to-date facts and stats, insight, humor, and a few fabulous recipes.

Gravity (2015)

They were the misfits and rabble-rousers — a small group of Army National Guardsmen from Tennessee, who, for as long as they could remember, had spent one weekend a month and two weeks each summer serving their country from the comforts of home.

In the aftermath of September 11, 2001, these citizen-soldiers were called into active duty, and were deployed to one of the most hostile regions in Iraq to fight a faceless enemy. Their most important mission was to make it home alive — until one day in August changed everything.

KENTUCKY BOURBON TOURS
Courtesy of Bourboncountry.com

BARDSTOWN and vicinity
  Barton's 1792 Distillery
  Heaven Hill Bourbon Heritage Center
  Limestone Branch Distillery
  Maker's Mark
  Willet Distillery
  Bardstown Bourbon Company
  Lux Row Distillers
  Preservation Distillery

BOWLING GREEN
  Corsair Artisan Distillery

DANVILLE
  Wilderness Trail Distillery
  Old Towne Distillery

FRANKFORT
  Buffalo Trace
  Castle & Key Distillery
  Three Boys Farm Distillery

LAWRENCEBURG
  Four Roses
  Wild Turkey

LEXINGTON and vicinity
  Barrel House Distilling Company
  Hartfield & Company Distillery
  Woodford Reserve
  Town Branch Distillery
  Bluegrass Distillers

LOUISVILLE and vicinity
    Angel's Envy Distillery
    LOUISVILLE and vicinity (continued)
    The Bulleit Experience at Stitzel-Weller
    Copper & Kings (Brandy aged in bourbon barrels)
    Evan Williams Bourbon Experience
    Grease Monkey Distillery at the Distilled Spirits
    Epicenter (classes only)
    Jefferson's Reserve at Kentucky Artisan Distillery
    Jim Beam Urban Stillhouse
    Kentucky Peerless Distilling Company.
    Old Forester Distillery (now open)
    Michter's Micro-Distillery (opening 2018 on Whiskey
Row)
    Rabbit Hole Distillery (now open)

NORTHERN KENTUCKY
    New Riff Distillery
    Old Pogue Distillery
    Boone County Distilling Company
    Neeley Family Distillery

WESTERN KENTUCKY
    MB Roland Distillery
    Casey Jones Distillery

SHELBYVILLE
    Jeptha Creed

SHEPHERDSVILLE
    Four Roses Warehouses & Bottling Tours
    Jim Beam American Stillhouse

PADUCAH
    Silent Brigade Distillery
    The Moonshine Company
EASTERN KENTUCKY
    Kentucky Mist Moonshine Distillery in Whitesburg

SUBSCRIBE

*Stay up to date on new releases, special offers,
and cool swag by subscribing to my email list.*

One of the best parts of being an author is getting to know my readers. I occasionally send out newsletters with updates on the latest books, special offers and new swag like the popular *Talk Bourbon to Me* t-shirts. You'll also be the first to know when *Talk Bourbon to Me 3* hits the shelves.

If you'd like to sign up, please visit talkbourbon.com

#talkbourbontome

ACKNOWLEDGMENTS

As one might expect, few projects are completed in solitude. Books are certainly no exception.

To every person featured in these pages, a million thanks for helping me bring this book into the material world. Being able tell your stories reinforces the reasons I love to write.

My editor and friend Joyce Gilmour is a saint. Thank you for putting up with my less-than-conventional methods. Marsha Hunt, Arlene Rattan, and Michelle Stevens: thank you for providing moral support when I needed it most, whether that meant accompanying me on distillery tours, trying out recipes, or providing an extra push forward. Darren Oliver, thanks for a great cover design. Thanks also to my Advance Reader Team, and to Stephen Scott, Randy Eisold, Michael Bounds, Jim Camp, and Ed Meredith for valuable input and enjoyable conversations. The bourbon industry will continue to thrive because of folks like you. See you at the distilleries!

ABOUT THE AUTHOR

Beth Underwood is an award-winning writer, alphabet juggler, and executive bourbon steward whose work has appeared in numerous newspapers, magazines, and books. An entertainer at heart, she enjoys writing about everyday life, finding sparks of sanity and comic relief in a world that sometimes seems to have gone berserk.

A Kentuckian for most of her life, she currently lives in the Bluegrass State with her son, their zany dog and a haughty cat. Her weekly columns appear in select Kentucky and Tennessee newspapers. Most days, she drinks her bourbon neat.

For more information:
Visit: bethwrightunderwood.com
Email: beth@bethwrightunderwood.com or
beth@talkbourbon.com
Instagram: @bethunderwoodbooks
Facebook: @talkbourbon and @bethunderwoodbooks